HAMLYN

# ROCK GARDEN FLOWERS

**A CONCISE GUIDE IN COLOUR**

# Rock Garden Flowers

*by Čestmír Böhm*

*Illustrated by Vindsor and Švarc*

*Hamlyn*
London · New York · Sydney · Toronto

Translated by Olga Kuthanová
Designed and Produced by Artia for
THE HAMLYN PUBLISHING GROUP LTD.
London • New York • Sydney • Toronto
Hamlyn House — The Centre — Feltham — Middlesex
© Copyright 1970 by Artia
Printed in Czechoslovakia
S 2578

# CONTENTS

Foreword
| | |
|---|---:|
| The Realm of Rock Plants | 9 |
| Before Building the Rock Garden | 11 |
| Construction of the Natural, Informal Rock Garden | 16 |
| The Formal Rock Garden, Wall and Terrace | 18 |
| The Rock Slope and Alpine Meadow in the Rock Garden | 22 |
| Planting Preparation | 25 |
| Selection, Planting and Cultivation of Rock Plants | 27 |
| Pools and Marshy Places in the Rock Garden | 31 |
| The Miniature Rock Garden | 35 |
| Plants for Sunny Positions | 36 |
| Shade for the Garden and Rock Garden | 39 |
| Hardy Ferns | 42 |
| Hardy Ornamental Grasses | 46 |
| Heathers | 48 |
| Propagation of Rock Plants | 51 |
| Small Bulbous and Tuberous Plants | 55 |
| Trees and Shrubs for the Rock Garden and Its Immediate Vicinity | 59 |
| Plates | 63 |
| Index of English names | 240 |
| Index of Latin names | 242 |

# FOREWORD

## The Realm of Rock Plants

The earliest gardens were in Ancient China and India; in Europe the Ancient Greeks and Romans were keen gardeners. Gardening was introduced into northern Europe by the Romans. During the Dark Ages only the monks kept herb gardens, in the 14th and 15th centuries there were many changes, now the common people had gardens too. For a long time the gardens were very formal, especially those of the very rich; in the 18th century, however, landscape gardening became popular influenced by men like 'Capability' Brown. Rock gardening was developed during the beginning of the 19th century, when many world famous rock gardens were laid out. Examples of these early gardens can be seen in the Royal Botanic Gardens at Kew, also at Edinburgh and Dublin.

Throughout the history of gardening many new plants, natives of various parts of the world, were introduced, also many new varieties of flowers and vegetables have been developed. Gradually the styles in gardening have changed and now rock gardens are very popular, and many varieties of alpine and other similar plants are available.

Many botanist-collectors have undertaken dangerous expeditions into the mountains, discovered and described new species of plants, then brought them back to their home countries and tried to acclimatize them. They learned the conditions under which the plants grew in the wild and tried to acquire an understanding of their life cycle. It is, thanks to the tireless efforts of these men, that today we can cultivate such a wide range of beautiful rock plants in our gardens.

Before this could come about, however, the plants had to become acclimatized to lower altitudes. This was a very difficult task and in the case of some species seemingly impossible. Growers of alpine plants, supplied from all over the world with specimens gathered by their collectors, did not achieve their first major successes till the end of the 19th century. They tried many plants to see which would grow in the new environment and above all experimented with hybridization, thus laying the foundation for their successful cultivation in gardens all over the world. It was discovered that at lower altitudes the cultivation of certain real high alpine species is very difficult and in some instances impossible. Only rarely will one find in our rock gardens such plants as the lovely Aretian Androsace *(Androsace helvetica)*, the spectacular *Phyteuma comosum* or the Jankea *(Jankea heldreichii)* of Greece, even though Androsaces from the Himalayas do very well here. Asiatic rock plants grow on much higher mountains than those in Europe but they are closer to the Equator, and so only those growing at elevations of more than 9,000 feet (3,000 metres) above sea level are hardy in our climate. In their natural habitat they have plenty of sun and often cold as well, with only a slight and inadequate covering of snow, the same as in Europe, besides being exposed to great variations in temperatures (day and night). For this reason these plants are remarkably hardy and are excellent for our rock gardens.

The growing of rock plants has become one of the most popular branches of gardening in recent years, for one can have a wide assortment of plants from almost the whole world in every, even the smallest rockery, be it in a corner of the garden, on a terrace, or level rooftop.

## Before Building the Rock Garden

The beauty of a rock garden depends on the wide diversity in size, shape and colour of the plants throughout the year. It remains a small oasis of colour even in the winter months, when its attractiveness is provided mainly by the evergreen plants. These include various Houseleeks *(Sempervivum)*, Rockfoils *(Saxifraga)*, Stonecrops *(Sedum)*, ornamental grasses, ferns, dwarf conifers, evergreen woody plants and many others. Then there are the species that bear flowers even in winter, e.g. Heathers *(Erica carnea)*, the Primrose *(Primula acaulis)*, the white Christmas Rose *(Helleborus niger)* and purple-red Lenten Rose *(H. atrorubens)*, and the fragrant *Daphne mezerum*. They are plants that are more or less indifferent to frost and the vagaries of the winter weather and are among the first in the garden to flower. These are followed by the early spring flowering species, by the bright colours of the bulbs, then by the varied hues of the summer flowerers and last of all by the interesting and rare blossoms of the autumn. In all, they embrace dozens of genera and hundreds of species.

In order to provide our rock plants with at least somewhat similar conditions to those of their natural habitat we plant them in rock gardens, thus achieving not only the required setting but first and foremost the prerequisites for the plants' healthy growth. Besides its suitable incorporation into the overall surroundings the natural arrangement of the rock garden will depend also on the best possible use of the local soil and climatic conditions. The natural environment which we have to take into account when building the rock garden also determines our choice of plants, for it is necessary to select such species as will do well without any specially taxing requirements as to cultivation. It is not advisable to grow too many kinds of plants in a small garden as each species requires different conditions for good health. In setting out the plants care should be taken to place the various types so that they harmonize and so that the vigorous growth of some will not crowd and destroy the beauty of the more delicate and precious species.

By planting the rockery with suitable alpines it is possible to obtain a natural effect, both in the natural rock garden built on a slope and in artificially constructed rock gardens built either on level ground, on a terrace or in the form of a wall. All depends on how well we manage to take advantage of the specific features of the various plants — their size, requirements as to position and soil, damp or dry environment, sun or semi-shade — as well as of the period of flowering and the individual colours of the blossoms, so as to achieve a beautiful and harmonious whole. Inspiration can always be sought in mother nature herself.

In order to enjoy our rock garden and achieve the best possible results, it is necessary to observe certain rules from the very begining. The first of these is the correct laying of the garden, which involves making the best use of the slope of the ground, selecting the correct position, and having a knowledge of the soil characteristics. Also of importance in making the rock garden a success is to select the proper species and varieties for the different parts of the rockery; it must never be over full, so that each plant may develop in all its beauty.

A rock garden may be laid, reconstructed, enlarged and planted at almost any time of the year, as long as the soil is sufficiently dry and can be handled with ease. It can also be placed almost anywhere, best of all, however, on a slope, in the sun as well as semi-shade, in any position and on any soil. By setting out suitable plants we can beautify even such spots which were formerly unsuitable even for grass. The rock garden should be built on different levels and with various nooks and crannies, so as to obtain the greatest possible number of sheltered spots facing various points of the compass, but at the same time protected from full sunlight, adverse conditions and severe frost.

One principle that should be kept in mind when

building the rockery is that a well constructed rock garden must be attractive even before planting. Much depends on the correct choice of stone. Indigenous rocks are the best, in other words rocks that are to be found in the surrounding countryside, both large and small, but always of the same kind. Very good and perhaps the prettiest is natural surface limestone covered with moss.

In connection with the laying of the rock garden one often hears of the various kinds of soils best suited for the different types of rock plants. Most of the common species will be satisfied with unfertilized normal garden soil, loamy-sandy with some humus, such as found in nature on hillsides or in fields. All that needs to be done is to prepare it carefully in dry weather, by removing all stubborn long-rooted weeds, and take care that other weeds do not invade the garden, especially those that are propagated by seed. For this reason the ground should be dug several times before the laying of the stones and planting and then weeded with care until the rock plants have spread. As soon as these have formed carpets, clumps and bushes that cover the ground, weeds will no longer establish themselves so easily.

To fulfill the special requirements of the more exacting species, it is wise to prepare beforehand coarse river sand which is used as drainage and finer sieved sand may be used as an admixture to special soil mixtures. It will also be necessary to have on hand sieved builder's rubble with a content of lime, compost, leaf mould, heath soil and peat as well as peat moss — *Sphagnum*. The best basis for all rock gardens is a neutral soil which can then be easily adapted according to need.

We must never use freshly fertilized soil, which is not beneficial to rock plants and in some instances might even be the direct cause of their improper growth or perhaps even death. Even so-called poor soils can be improved by adding natural humus, leaf-mould, peat, heath soil or compost, always with an admixture of sand, to the whole area of the rock garden. Otherwise humus is added only for certain more exacting plants. On the other hand soils that are too rich in humus are adapted according to need by adding sand. In the case of species with silvery or felted foliage, e.g. the Mouse-ear Chickweeds *(Cerastium)*, Wormwoods *(Artemisia)* and Edelweiss *(Leontopodium)*, it is necessary to add also sieved builder's rubble, thereby ensuring that these plants will retain their compact growth and characteristic colour of the leaves. Lime in any form should never be put over the whole of the rock garden but only given to certain lime-loving plants, for otherwise those rock plants that do not tolerate lime would succumb and their successful cultivation would be impossible. These include the lovely ericaceous plants, certain Heathers *(Calluna, Erica)*, Azaleas, Rhododendrons, *Kalmia* and others which, with a few exceptions, are all calcifuge and a *must* in every rock garden.

Before commencing with the construction of the rock garden beginners should know why they want to build a rockery, what they expect of it, and above all if they also want some trees, ornamental shrubs, flower or vegetable beds and some grass in their garden. In that case it is necessary to keep in mind that the rockery requires a suitable position with adequate sun and air, both important factors for the successful growth of most rock plants. However, shaded places should be provided as well, for the woodland and other shade-loving plants, and last of all it is necessary for the rockery to form a part from the rest of the garden and placed so that it harmonizes with its environment.

## Construction of the Natural, Informal Rock Garden

The rules and suggestions on how to build a rock garden are many. One can never go wrong, however, in taking a look at mother nature, at the arrangement of rocks and boulders in the wild, and at the successful rock gardens of one or more alpine growers which can serve as an example for the construction of one's own. As we have already said, a well built rockery must be attractive even before planting and the grown plants must never completely conceal or cover the stones, which not only provide the necessary environment for the plants but are also an important decorative element in themselves.

Unless it is laid on naturally sloping ground, the rock garden is built up on and around the so-called supporting structure. For this one can use various kinds of builder's rubble, small stones, gravel, clinker, bricks, boulders, etc. These are piled up on the spot selected for the rockery, thus forming a loose, porous and at the same time firm foundation, which after being roughly shaped in the desired contours is covered with loose, clean soil, free of weeds. Then follows the actual placing of the stones and final shaping of the rock garden.

If building on a natural slope or hillock we begin at the bottom, trying to place the individual rocks, which should be of various sizes, as well as groups of rocks so that they will retain the soil on the slope and prevent it from being washed down by the rain. The stones are arranged in irregular formation to create large and smaller spaces to receive the various plants. In doing so it is well to know beforehand where we plan to place the individual species. The stones should never be piled to form a hillock rising abruptly from level ground, for this has an unnatural and artifical look. Is is better to use a few larger rocks and boulders arranged to give a natural effect, placed in shaded spots where rock plants would not thrive. They should be embedded firmly in the ground, with the aid of a hand trowel or small spade, two-thirds below and one-third above the surface of the soil. They should always be laid on the broadest side, never pointing upward. It is also possible to arrange several smaller stones to look like a large boulder, at the same time providing a large number of spaces and joins suitable for the planting of certain small plants. When laying the stones it is well to remember to include several 'stepping' stones — preferably flat ones — for moving about in and tending the rock garden. The rockery should have a natural appearance. This is achieved by proper construction and by the arrangement of the plants, especially by the use of various dwarf shrubs, low grasses, small ferns, etc.

If the ground on which we want to build the rockery is flat, differences in level can be achieved by excavation in certain places or by making sunken paths around the future rockery and distributing the soil thus gained in uneven layers over the space where the rocks will be laid. Never, under any circumstances, should artifical mounds or hillocks be made on flat ground, for these can never create a natural effect. It is better to use only a few large boulders placed singly or in groups in the shaded or partially shaded parts of the garden with a large number of certain woodland plants planted in between, so that they can spread freely.

# The Formal Rock Garden, Wall and Terrace

Small, irregular areas, especially in the middle of a town, are not suitable for the natural type of garden. Here it is best to build one or more low walls joined, if desired, by terraces. Such walls and terraces linking up with the house or garden steps should have simple and efficient lines. Variously placed walls and terraces facing in all directions provide a large number of spaces, narrow crevices, pockets and other sites for the flourishing growth of the plants.

Large gardens with steeply sloping ground are also difficult to cultivate and so here, too, terraces provide the ideal solution. Walls with beds at the foot and on top are very decorative, easy to tend and plant, and serve to keep the soil and its nutrients from being washed away.

The edges of terraces and walls can be planted with rock plants that flower at different times, both those in sunny positions, as well as those facing away from the sun or in partial shade. Good protection against the washing off of soil by heavy rains is achieved by the planting of certain exceptionally persistent plants such as the low, shrubby Asters *(Aster dumosus)* perennial Pinks *(Dianthus)*, Catchfly *(Viscaria)*, Thrifts *(Armeria)*, Catmint *(Nepeta)*, Mouse-ear Chickweeds *(Cerastium)* and Lavender *(Lavandula)*. Also very good in sunny terrace beds are the profuse blossoms of roses, in places where previously only weeds and wild shrubs would grow.

If the garden, or at least part of it, is situated on a slope, it is well to take advantage of this to build one or, in the case of steeper slopes, several walls, combined, perhaps, with paths and steps to provide easy access to all parts of the garden.

When erecting fairly low walls the stones are generally not joined by cement but by filling the gaps with carefully sieved, slightly sandy soil with some humus. The wall stones used should be of different sizes, unhewn or partly hewn, but always of the same kind.

A well established and correctly constructed wall should be inclined backwards, not only to hold up the bank better but also so that the rain will be directed into the soil and retained there for the plants. In placing the stones it is necessary to remember to make smaller and larger gaps for the planting of certain species. The bottom layer of stones should be partially buried to form a secure base for the wall. This is then further strengthened by the root system of the rock plants and dwarf conifers planted there.

Dry walls can be combined with an informal rockery or a pool edged with stone. Paved paths alongside borders, beneath walls or terrace steps are also very attractive, however, stones that are not flat enough make walking unpleasant. In that case it is far better to use slabs of concrete buried in the ground and edged with carpeting rock plants, especially such species that are not harmed by being stepped on, e.g. the modest *Cotula squalida*, the interesting, low growing Whitlow Wort *(Paronychia)*, the fragrant Thyme *(Thymus)*, Pearlwort *(Sagina subulata)*, certain Stonecrops *(Sedum)* and many other low growing plants.

Best for planting in walls in the sun are hanging cushion plants and shrub plants such as Purple Rock Cress *(Aubrieta)*, Rock Jasmine *(Androsace)*, Mouse-ear Chickweed *(Cerastium)*, *Bahia*, Chalk Plant *(Gypsophila)*, Sun Rose *(Helianthemum)*, Asters, Pinks *(Dianthus)*, Madwort *(Alyssum)*, Evening Primrose *(Oenothera)*, Candytuft *(Iberis)*, Rock Cress *(Arabis)*, *Tunica* and countless other species and varieties that are long lived, and when properly selected will provide colour with their blossoms throughout the whole growing period.

The sheltered and damper spots at the foot of the wall are just the place for the Primulas and related plants. Excellent for the top of the wall in full sun are the vast clumps of the downy Pasque Flower *(Pulsatilla)*, fine-leaved Pheasant's Eye *(Adonis vernalis)* Dragons' heads *(Dracocephallum)* and scented *Daphne cneorum*. In larger terraces there is usually room also for several shrubs and conifers, e.g. *Cotoneaster*, Barberries *(Berberis)*, the dwarf or prostrate Junipers *(Juniperus communis* 'Hibernica' or *Juniperus sabina)* and similar woody plants. It is always necessary, however, to take into account the area required by the plants for their growth and to space them accordingly.

For higher walls that are difficult to cover adequately for the winter good plants are the prostrate Phloxes *(Phlox subulata)*, Purple Rock Cress *(Aubrieta)*, Madwort *(Alyssum)*, Wormwood *(Artemisia)*, Pinks *(Dianthus)*, Spurges *(Euphorbia)*, Soapworts *(Saponaria)* and Rockfoils *(Saxifraga)*, which flower in spring. Summer flowerers are the golden St. John's Wort *(Hypericum)*, Bell Flowers *(Campanula)* and double *Tunica saxifraga* 'Rosette', bearing flowers continually almost until winter; also Savory *(Satureia)*, Campion *(Silene)*, Stonecrop *(Sedum)*, Aster and certain summer Gentians *(Gentiana)*.

These walls are the framework for different combinations of plants and colours that are not found in the rockery and the garden thus gains in its dimensions of colour and greenery.

Plants can be set out in dry walls practically throughout the whole year. Those that have been cultivated in flowerpots before setting out in the garden are more likely to become well established quickly and take root. After putting the plant in its predetermined spot in the wall, it should be secured with some moss, best of all peat moss, which provides good protection against sun and maintains constant moisture, especially during the critical period until it is well rooted.

## The Rock Slope and Alpine Meadow in the Rock Garden

Experienced growers often attempt to grow rock plant species that normally do not thrive in the usual garden and under the usual conditions. These plants have special requirements, for in their native habitat many of them occur at high altitudes, even near the edge of the permanent ice and snow. In this case it is necessary to build a special rockery or else a special section in the normal rock garden which would attempt to resemble the plant's natural environment. It is necessary to provide greater differences in height, either by making a sort of rock slope or a cliff comprised of a greater number of stones to gain as many joins and crevices as possible as well as, and above all, cooler sites which may be exposed to the sun for a while (most alpine plants do not tolerate permanent shade), but will be sheltered from the noonday sun.

An excellent effect is obtained by creating the equivalent of a small alpine meadow at the foot of the slope, either alone or combined with a small pool or bog. When building the rock slope it is necessary to keep in mind what plants are to be placed there, in other words the purpose it is to serve. The large stones, therefore, must not be laid too close together, but in such a way as to leave gaps filled with soil and small stones to provide the most suitable environment for many precious, delicate and truly beautiful rock plants. It is also necessary to remember to make some larger pockets for the planting of several dwarf shrubs to give this section a natural look.

Sites suitable for the planting of ferns and other shade-loving plants should always be shaded from the sun. This will then guarantee the successful growth of the rare Pyrenean Primrose *(Ramonda pyrenaica* syn. *R. myconi)* and closely related plants such as *Haberlea* and *Jankea*. Good companions for these rare plants are *Soldanella* a very attractive spring flowerer with violet tinted, fringed bells, the white *Moehringia muscosa*, *Androsace lactea*, as well as Rockfoils of the section Porphyrion-*Saxifraga oppositifolia*.

Besides the rare and precious alpines the sunny positions of the rock slope could be planted also with Pasque Flowers *(Pulsatilla)*. Not to be neglected are other typical representatives of the mountain flora such as the Bell Flowers *(Campanula)*, certain low growing Primulas, Whitlow Grass *(Draba)* and the continually flowering Alpine Poppies *(Papaver alpinum)* which tend to sow themselves freely and thus spread to most parts of the rock garden.

The sides of the rock slope should be planted with suitable species, keeping in mind their special requirements as to sun and shade, dryness and moisture, given by the conditions of their natural habitat. A basic requirement to keep in mind is that this special rockery should not be erected in the shadow of a house, a wall or tall trees; the cooler situations being attained not by shade, but by creating many and diversely arranged spaces.

The alpine meadow, at the foot of the slope, should always be of sufficient size to fulfill the natural requirements of the plants grown there. First of all it is necessary to prepare a shallow hollow with compacted clay or other impervious material as base, covered with a layer of peat and sand and topped with a layer of soil mixture consisting of well-rotted compost, some peat and sand. Uneven ground, raised slightly here and there, provides a suitable environment for many rock plants, some of which would not thrive in the normal rock garden. A pleasant oasis in any rockery, the alpine meadow is excellent for such plants as the Bird's Eye Primrose *(Primula farinosa)* and *Primula longiflora*, Butterworts *(Pinguicula)*, Grass of Parnassus *(Parnassia)* and small shrubs, e.g. dwarf Rhododendrons. Also suitable are the low Alpine Buttercups, blue Spring Gentian *(Gentiana verna)*, the interesting Felwort *(Swertia)*, the liliaceous Bog Asphodels *(Asphodelus palustris)* and other alpines with similar requirements.

Indispensable for giving the alpine meadow a natural look are certain low and non-invasive grasses which are, moreover, good foils for all the plants grown in this part of the rockery.

# Planting Preparation

To be assured of the successful growth of the plants it is necessary to know the conditions in which they grow in the wild, especially in the case of the more precious species. It is therefore recommended to keep one's eyes open when going to the mountains or for a walk and note the arrangement of the ground, the situation of each species, the type of soil and the entire plant community, i.e. the natural neighbours of the given species. Good knowledge of these factors is one of the chief prerequisites for success in cultivation especially of the most exacting and thus also the rarest types of rock plants.

If on the lookout for it, valuable information is to be found not only in the high mountains but also on hills, slopes, woodlands, and even shrub-covered banks and meadows in valleys, sometimes often quite close to where we live.

It is also necessary to realize that in our lowland gardens many rock plants are already in bloom while the mountains are still covered with a thick blanket of snow. In other words, the growing period of high alpines in cultivation is several weeks longer than in the wild. The two to four months difference is not in the least benefitial for certain truly high altitude plants and it is necessary to keep this in mind when selecting their site in the rockery.

Also of importance for successful cultivation in our gardens is the place of origin of the various species. The early and attractive Rockfoil *(Saxifraga oppositifolia)* never has such a profusion of flowers in the garden as in the mountains; its more southern form *Saxifraga oppositifolia* var. *latina* from the Apennine Mountains of Italy, on the other hand, grows very well and has a wealth of blossoms.

These Rockfoils, the same as all high alpines, require a special position in the rockery, best of all facing east but turned away from the sun. It is recommended to put them in small rock fissures and crevices in porous soil, continually supplied with an adequate amount of water, mixed with coarse sand or small stones, some peat and clay. Only under these conditions will the plants reward us with thriving growth and attractive floral display.

Similar parts of the rock garden can be planted with other cold-loving plants, but only species that are of compact and not invasive habit. They must also complement one another as regards appearance, even though they include carpeting plants, cushion plants and shrubs. However, not all mountain rock plants like cold. A position in full sun is welcomed by the Edelweiss *(Leontopodium)*, the low-growing Aster-like *Townsendia*, from the Rocky Mountains, *Edraianthus* and certain Bell Flowers *(Campanula)*.

The soil for high altitude plants must never be enriched with natural or artifical fertilizers. In the wild they have only a little natural humus and remain in one place for many years, sometimes even decades. Their vitality, hardiness and persistence is truly remarkable.

Garden forms as well as most species growing at lower altitudes have greater requirements as regards the amount of nourishment in the soil. Therefore, if need be, it can be enriched with well-rotted compost, but only in such a quantity that will not upset the plants' balanced growth; they might lose their resistance to disease and frost and in many instances might not flower at all or only sparsely.

Most of the above points refer to the rare and therefore also more exacting species. The usual rock plants, which as a rule far outnumber the precious species in the garden, are generally very modest and undemanding, but beautiful and attrative all the same, and are content with almost any situation and whatever soil is available in the garden.

## Selection, Planting and Cultivation of Rock Plants

Rock plants are planted and transplanted primarily in spring. However, those grown in flowerpots can be set out at any time in the growing period. The most difficult task for every beginner is the selection of suitable species, for catalogues and specialized literature tempt him with hundreds of different species, varieties and forms.

The first ones to be planted in the rock garden are those plants which are the hardiest, have great vitality and are pleasing to the eye, especially if planted in large numbers. They include many species that can grow well in comparatively poor and dry soil and a position in full sun. Worthy of particular note are the grey-leaved Mouse-ear Chickweeds *(Cerastium)* which make rich carpets, the cushiony, prostrate *Phlox subulata* (syn. *Phlox setacea)* covered with thousands of pink, red, violet or white stars in the flowering period, the well known golden Madwort *(Alyssum saxatile)*, the low-growing carpeting Purple Rock Cress *(Aubrieta)* with flowers of various shades, the Pinks *(Dianthus)*, Rock Cress *(Arabis)*, Thyme *(Thymus)*, as well as Thrift *(Armeria)*, Bell Flowers *(Campanula)*, Wormwood *(Artemisia)*, Speedwell *(Veronica)*, and other small yet very attractive rock plants. However, even in the case of these undemanding plants it is of course necessary after a time to improve the soil by occasional aerating and adding more nourishing soil, rotted turf with leaf mould and well rotted compost.

When planting it is necessary to select the species so as to ensure continual flowering in the rock garden, one species after the other throughout the year. It is also possible to select such an assortment that will provide a fine floral display at a specific time, when one can enjoy it most. More experienced growers can also plant the rarer rock plants which often prolong the floral display of the rock garden or enhance it with the special beauty of alpine blossoms. These more demanding plants, however, require not only the preparation of a suitable position but also of suitable soil with good drainage.

Every beginner should first learn to know and appreciate the beauty of rock plants, which as a rule do not have such striking blooms as the rose, *Dahlia* or *Chrysanthemum*. Their attraction lies in their simple beauty, elegant shape of the flowers and perfect harmony of the plant as a whole.

Small, high alpines are best planted in greater numbers to be more effective. The more common species which take root easily and have a good root system can be grown in open ground in beds. Others are cultivated in pots which assures their successful rooting and allows them to be planted out at almost any time of the year.

Planting is best done with a trowel or dibber. The plants are set firmly in the soil and then watered thoroughly. In dry weather the surface can be covered with additional loose soil which will retain the required moisture for a longer period. Certain more demanding plants, such as cushion Saxifrages (Kabschias Section), are top dressed with small stones, others such as the Pinks *(Dianthus alpinus)* or certain Bell Flowers e.g. *Campanula bellidifolia* as well as all species of Bitterroot *(Lewisia)* must also be protected with small stones.

The rock garden should be watered as needed. In dry weather the plants, especially those recently planted out, should be watered every day, in the morning and evening. Care, however, must be taken not to overdo it, for excessive moisture is more harmful than drought. Further care of the garden includes occasional aerating of the soil and removal of weeds. Annual weeds are no problem, but perennials are more difficult, as it is necessary to remove the stubborn roots as well. However, as soon as the rock plants have spread and covered the ground, the danger of weeds is no longer so great.

Protection is needed from the cold winter winds and frosts. Survival also depends in large measure on proper care throughout the growing period. Only healthy and hardy plants can hope to survive the vagaries of winter without harm.

Mountain plants, especially high alpines, are in a state of rest underneath a thick layer of snow throughout almost the whole of the long winter in their natural habitat. It is therefore necessary to provide them with a winter cover in our gardens, even when there is no snow. Certain rock plants appreciate a top dressing of mossy peat in winter or a ground cover of leaves weighted down with a layer of branches. In situations where there is danger of continual damp, certain species will do better if provided with faultless drainage. This should be kept in mind when planting, and also if they are covered with panes of glass, transparent foil, etc. for protection. This is required by Bitter-root *(Lewisia)*, Horned Rampion *(Phyteuma comosum)*, *Cyclamen coum*, *Incarvillea* and other rock plants with similar requirements. Some other rock plants will benefit by a light cover of branches or bracken. However, plants should not be covered until the first hard frost so that they will not rot in their shelters during rainy weather and also so as not to provide a haven for mice, which may eat many bulbous plants.

Rock plants require care even in winter time. It is necessary to check them in their shelters now and then to make sure that no danger threatens, especially in warmer, rainy weather which is conducive to mould.

Premature uncovering of the plants in early spring is also inadvisable. It is best to wait until the weather becomes settled and then remove the covering, preferably on a colder day. This covering should be kept on hand, however, in case the weather takes an unexpected turn for the worse and there is danger of dry frost.

On removing the protective covering, it is necessary to check all those plants that were planted out in autumn. If they have been pulled up by the frost it is necessary to make them firm, cover with soil and water them so that they do not become too dry. The next task is to clean and tidy up the rock garden, cut off the dried stems, aerate the soil and add soil where it has been washed away. However, care must be taken not to damage the sprouting bulbs.

# Pools and Marshy Places in the Rock Garden

The beauty of every garden can be enhanced by a stream, pool, pond or small lake suitably set in the immediate surroundings. These may be geometrical or of irregular shapes, shallow or deep. Rock gardeners will enjoy even a small pool placed in the rock garden itself, with one or two vertical walls jutting up above the water and covered with appropriate pendant plants. These rock plants do very well in a sunny position with adequate atmospheric moisture.

The pool in the natural rock garden should have an irregular contour. It may be fairly deep in the centre but with shallower edges to permit the cultivation of the interesting marsh plants. The slopes of the rock garden should be arranged so that excess water, both when it rains and when watering, flows into the pool, thus keeping it at the required level. The edges of the pool should be carefully masked by suitably placed rocks, sand and above all by plants naturally found in this type of environment. At the same time it is necessary to remember that the basin is made chiefly of cement, which is not permeable to water, and to select the plants accordingly, namely xerophilous species — however, we mustn't forget to water them.

The basin should be lined with a thick layer of concrete reinforced with wire. Another possibility is to install a prefabricated plastic basin or polythene sheeting in the excavated ground. The edges of the pool must be at the same level so that they are uniformly covered by the water, but the shape can be any the gardener desires, always keeping in mind, however, that the basin must broaden out towards the top so that the walls will not be damaged by ice.

Basins in which water-lilies are to be grown must be at least 20 to 34 inches (50 to 80 cm.) deep, for these plants must be continually submerged in water during the growing period. They are planted either directly into nourishing soil at the bottom of the pool or into baskets, boxes or other containers. These are lined, both sides and bottom, with moss, then the sides with half-rotted cow dung, and the remainder filled in with clayey soil mixed with well rotted natural manure. The water-lily is then inserted up to its neck and the whole container may be covered with moss and dry fir branches or bracken, anchored with zinc-coated wire mesh to prevent the water washing off the nourishing soil. Thus prepared, the container with the water-lily can be dropped to the bottom of the pool.

Growing water-lilies is not difficult, requiring chiefly calm, quiet water and plenty of sun. The water in the pool should be on the soft side, best of all is rain water or else tap water that has been allowed to stand for some time to remove the chlorine. If other water plants are set out in the pool as well, then it is advisable to stock it also with small fish which will destroy the mosquito larvae. So that the plants might survive the winter without harm, the pool should be sufficiently deep to prevent it completely freezing up when properly covered. With the onset of the first severe frosts a wooden cover should be laid over the surface of the pool and this should be topped with at least an 8 inch (20 cm.) layer of leaves. If the water-lilies are planted in pots, these can be removed from the water and stored in a cold but not freezing room, to be put back again in spring.

Water-lilies can be planted in April and on through the whole summer if they have been pre-cultivated in pots. Propagation is by the division of older plants in spring; those with small leaves and no longer bearing blossoms will greatly benefit by this and by being transplanted into fresh, nourishing soil with a small amount of bone meal.

The shallow parts of pools, bogs, as well as the damp banks of streams and ponds are especially suitable for growing the interesting marsh plants such as the Yellow Flag *(Iris pseudoacorus)*, Arrowhead

*(Sagittaria)*, ornamental marsh grasses — *(Glyceria aquatica* 'Variegata') or Rushes *(Juncus)* — as well as the single and double Marsh Marigolds *(Caltha palustris)*, Bog Arum *(Calla palustris)* and other plants.

Slightly marshy margins are suitable for Butterworts *(Pinguicula)*, the Bird's Eye Primrose *(Primula farinosa* or *Primula rosea)*, and Grass of Parnassus *(Parnassia)*. The soil for these plants should be fairly heavy, well ripened, loose, with an addition of clay and a porous sandy foundation. They also like peat with humus. However, soil from streams or natural bogs is not recommended, for this may introduce various diseases, pests and aquatic weeds into our garden.

Larger pools and other areas which are moist in summer, but not continually covered by water, and dry in winter are also good for the successful cultivation of certain Irises, the most fascinating being the Japanese Iris *(Iris kaempferi)* in many different colours, also the Siberian Iris *(Iris sibirica)* and *Iris graminea*, unusually hardy and persistent plants. Very attractive perennials for these parts of the garden are the Goat's Beards *(Astilbe)* with their graceful plumes of small flowers in shades of white, pink and red.

Further good waterside plants are the many kinds of Primulas, including the Asiatic species such as *Primula japonica*, Windflowers or Anemones *(Anemone japonica* and *Anemone vitifolia)* the various garden forms of Spiderwort *(Tradescantia virginiana)* as well as Orchids, the Water Forget-me-not *(Myosotis palustris)* and Globe Flowers *(Trollius)* or Meadow Rues *(Thalictrum)*.

The tiny crevices in the rocks above the water can be filled with small Saxifrages and ferns, e.g. Spleenworts or Rues, and also with south European and Alpine Bell Flowers, that have an almost continual flowering period.

## The Miniature Rock Garden

A miniature rock garden can be built in the usual window box or wooden troughs of various dimensions. The drainage hole at the bottom should be covered with perforated zinc so that it does not become blocked, thus permitting the drainage of excess water. The lower third of the container is covered with fine gravel and coarse sand as drainage, and this is topped with a soil mixture of clean soil, free of weeds, peat, well rotted compost, old mortar and sand. This is filled up to the rim, watered and allowed to settle for several days. Only then are the contours of the rock garden designed and the stones laid as in the normal rockery, positioning them to create rock joins and sheltered sites for the more demanding rock plants. In very small window boxes the small stones are put in place after the planting.

Plants that do not tolerate lime should be put in special containers bedded in soil, consisting of peat, heath soil, garden soil and sand.

Rock gardens can be built in a similar manner on balconies, terraces or flat roofs. Many home cultivators and admirers of the miniature rock garden quite possibly also have a normal rockery in the garden, or else grow alpines in large flower pots, bowls, small troughs or large ones hewn out of big boulders.

These various arrangements can be placed in the garden, on the terrace in front of the house, beside steps, in front of a summer alcove, beside a bench, in short, wherever they can be seen often. They are particularly effective against the background of ornamental evergreen trees and shrubs and are best placed on the east or west side of the house, the south side having too much sun, although even this position can be planted with situable sun-loving species.

When planting miniature rock gardens we must follow the same rules as in the normal rockery. In addition to this all parts of the miniature rock garden can be supplemented with a rich assortment of small bulbous and tuberous plants, which are among the first to flower and whose lovely floral display is not only a welcome herald of spring but also a rich and colourful addition to the rock garden at this time of the year.

## Plants for Sunny Positions

In some gardens there are parts which are not easy to design and cannot be planted with the usual cultivated species. These may be steep slopes, banks, or similar places where the soil is so poor that even normal grass has a hard time keeping a foothold and dries up in the summer heat, especially where exposed to direct sun. And yet there are plants that are not only an excellent substitute for grass but will make these inhospitable parts of the garden truly attractive. Foremost of the undemanding plants that thrive in the heat of the sun are the somewhat neglected Mouse-ear Chickweeds *(Cerastium)*. The taller growing species are planted in larger spaces, whereas the daintier ones with their low, thick, whitish-green mats are excellent fillers of dry spots in the smaller rock garden.

The commonly grown species such as *Cerastium biebersteinii* and *C. tomentosum* var. *columnae* do very well in dry, sunny positions in larger rock gardens. They are also suitable as border plants for flower beds alongside paths and especially for strengthening slopes and banks facing south. Compact growth and rich white foliage is best assured by planting them in poor, dry soil.

During the flowering period, in May and June, the Mouse-ear Chickweeds are covered with a profusion of white blossoms. Soon after flowering it is necessary to remove the seeds and top dress the plants with loose, sandy soil.

Further true xerophilous plants are the Wormwoods *(Artemisia)*, which do exceptionally well on poor soils. They have either silvery or green foliage and are very hardy, standing up to all kinds of weather. In the wild, e.g. in the limestone Alps, they are the most popular of the mountain plants, together with the Edelweiss.

Best suited to our gardens are the low, silver-leaved *Artemisia lanata* a native of the Dolomites, *A. mutelina* from central and southern Europe and the fresh green *A. nana*. Because the flowers are not particularly pretty and are of little account they should be removed as soon as they appear, so that the plants will make nice, compact mats.

Very attractive on the sloping ground of the rock garden at all times of the year are certain grasses such as *Festuca alpina*, *F. amethystina*, *F. glacialis*, *F. glauca*, *F. scoparia* and other low-growing species as well as certain ornamental thistles, e.g. the Silver Thistle *(Carlina acaulis)* with its silvery-grey rosettes and other xerophilous plants suitably set out amidst the low, carpeting alpines to break the monotony of a single planting.

Also good for these positions are certain small shrubs such as *Cotoneaster* and *Berberis*, and of the small conifers chiefly the prostrate Junipers, such the Common Savin *(Juniperus sabina* 'Tamariscifolia'*)* and the like.

The best plants for those parts of the rock garden comprising light-coloured stones are species with dark green foliage, resistant to sun and drought of course, and for the parts consisting of dark coloured stones ones with grey, silvery or grey-green foliage, which, however, must not predominate. When the grey-leaved plants spread they make whole carpets and form an effective contrast to the dark stones.

Stone crevices and small spaces in sunny situations are effectively planted with various species of Stonecrop *(Sedum)* and whole groups of Houseleek *(Sempervivum)*. If there is a situation in full sun which has porous soil with a slight content of lime and an admixture of clay and sand it is possible to successfully cultivate hardy Prickly Pears *(Opuntias)*. There are many more plants commonly grown in the garden that are suitable for planting on slopes and rock gardens in the sun. These include the perennial Pinks *(Dianthus)*, Chalk Plants *(Gypsophila)*, Purple Rock Cress *(Aubrieta)* Madwort *(Alyssum)*, Thyme *(Thymus)* and others that flourish and do well in such places.

# Shade for the Garden and Rock Garden

Some gardens, especially old well established ones, have many shaded places, which can be used to advantage for plants that either like partial shade or else tolerate complete shade very well. The degree of shade varies, and in order to select the most suitable species for the given spot it is necessary to assess the shade correctly, both as to density and duration, for the latter also has considerable influence on the growth of the plant.

The soil in these shady situations can always be improved; it is even possible to achieve a sufficiently thick layer of humus. Certain older trees, such as Elms, Ashes, Birches and Maples, however, soon spread their roots even in this layer of loose soil thus using up the moisture and food material it contains, leaving only slight nourishment for the small plants and causing poor growth and tiny flowers.

It is interesting that almost all the so-called shade-loving plants like some light and their growth endeavours to reach it. The well known Ivy *(Hedera helix)*, for instance, although planted in the shade always tries to climb upward towards the light, where it spreads its blossoms. The beautiful *Clematis alpina* of the European Alps and *C. macropetala* of the Himalayas, both love shade on their roots but grow towards the light and thrive best and flower in full sun.

Most woodland plants, both in the wild and in the ordinary garden or rock garden, flower before the leaves of the surrounding trees have emerged to shade them. Many lovely woodland plants grow and flower better at the edges of the wood than in the full shade of the shrubs and trees. Today's growers also cultivate many species formerly considered as strictly shade-loving plants, with far greater success in the sun. These include, for instance, the Lilies-of-the-Valley *(Convallaria majalis)* and the Primulas, which under certain conditions are healthy, strong and lovely even in sunny situations.

We must not, however, consider those plants that are grown on north-facing banks or in dry walls turned away from the sun as shade plants, because they can also be grown in sunny positions, but do not grow well in dry conditions and in direct sun; they must be supplied with sufficient water during the growing season. Thus, as often happens, such plants as the Pyrenean Primrose *(Ramonda)*, *Haberlea* and similar species should not be classed as shade-loving, the same being true of certain *Bergenias* and mountain ferns, e.g. the Shield Fern *(Polystichum lonchitis)*, which do quite well in partial shade, but are far more beautiful in the sun.

Slightly semi-shady positions can be planted with

a wide variety of perennials and other rock plants that thrive in every good garden soil. These include also various Saxifrages and Pinks *(Dianthus plumarius)*, in other words plants that are often grown also in sunny situations. It is interesting that sometimes, even though they do well in such parts of the garden, they do not bear as many flowers as in the sun.

Many interesting and pretty flowering perennials can be grown as ground cover in partial shade under taller trees or shrubs. This list includes, the Bugle *(Ajuga)* in its cultivated forms, Lady's Mantle *(Alchemilla acutiloba)*, Snake Root or Wild Ginger *(Asarum europaeum)*, various species of Anemones *(Anemone)*, *Bergenia*, Lilies-of-the-Valley *(Convallaria)*, Yellow Fumitory *(Corydalis lutea)*, Goat's Beard *(Astilbe chinensis* 'Pumila'*)*, Barrenwort *(Epimedium)* in its cultivated forms, various ferns, Hepaticas *(Hepatica triloba)*, Plantain Lily in its cultivated forms *(Hosta* syn. *Funkia)*, Navelwort *(Omphalodes verna)*, Alleghany spurge *(Pachysandra terminalis)*, Knotgrass *(Polygonum affine)*, various species of *Primula*, Lungwort *(Pulmonaria)* mossy and leathery Saxifrages *(Saxifraga)*, Foam Flower *(Tiarella cordifolia)*, Dwarf Periwinkle *(Vinca minor)*, *Waldsteinia* and also certain sedges *(Carex)* and ornamental grasses such as *Luzula silvatica*.

In densely shaded places we can plant the Common Wild Woodruff *(Asperula odorata)* which spreads well even under tall conifers and is very effective also under large ferns. It bears a profusion of not very large white flowers and forms thick, bright green mats in places where other plants will not grow.

# Hardy Ferns

Ferns, which differ to a certain extent from other plants, are very interesting to many gardeners. Their graceful fronds and interesting shapes make them a welcome addition to the garden and rockery.

The vigorous growth of various species of ferns in the woods catch the eye on walks in summer, especially at higher elevations. The partially shaded parts of the garden are also enhanced by the beauty of ferns and they are good companions for many shade-loving plants.

Very effective, especially in spring, are the yellow-green growths of the Ostrich Fern *(Matteucia struthiopteris* formerly known by the name of *Struthiopteris germanica)*. This fern reaches a height of nearly 3 feet (80 cm.) and it thrives both in shade and in the sun, best in a moist situation.

The North American Maidenhair *(Adiantum pedatum)* has the appearance of a hot-house fern. Its black, wiry stems, up to 20 inches (50 cm.) high, are covered with delicate pale green foliage. It likes semi-shady to fully shaded positions and the company of attractive perennials, such as the spring flowering Primulas and Anemones, the Carpathian Bell Flowers, the low-growing Goat's Beard *(Astilbe)* and Meadow Saffron *(Colchicum autumnale)*. They appreciate a not too dry, loose and slightly acidic soil with humus.

The Bladder Fern *(Cystopteris bulbifera)* is another fern grown in our gardens. It attains a height of about 16 inches (40 cm.) and is the hardiest of this group along with *Cystopteris fragilis*. It does very well in shaded positions in damp, stony soil.

Another ornamental fern is the Sensitive Fern *(Onoclea sensibilis)* with its triangular, pale green bipinnate, about 2 to 3 feet (80 cm.) long foliage. It spreads with ease and is content with almost any position in the garden, doing well even in the sun, especially on a north-facing bank. This slightly primeval-looking fern likes damp soil and will grow even in shallow water. The plant forms underground shoots, by which it can be propagated. As companions we can plant also certain more precious and unusual plants such as the Wood Lily *(Trillium grandiflorum)* of North America or Merry Bells *(Uvularia grandiflora)*, another lilaceous plant of the same origin, as well as the May Apple *(Podophyllum emodi)* of the Himalayas.

The popular Hart's Tongue Fern *(Phyllitis scolopendrium* syn. *Scolopendrium vulgare)* is an interesting species with smooth, undivided leaves, requiring lime in the soil. In the wild it grows in stony woodlands in damp, rocky shaded situations occurring in the lowlands and up to elevations of 6,000 feet (2,000 metres). Its long tongue-shaped leaves grow to a length of 16 inches (40 cm.) and have elongate sori on the undersurface. The Hart's Tongue Fern is also lovely in heavily shaded and damp parts of the garden or rock garden. It should always be planted between stones, which it prefers. There are several forms of this species with variously frilled leaves; in *P. scolopendrium* 'Cristatum' the tips of the leaves are markedly cleft. These ferns are very effective planted between Shooting-Star *(Dodecatheon)*, *Cortusa*, Toothwort *(Dentaria)* or *Soldanella montana*.

The Adder's Fern *(Polypodium vulgare)* is a flat-spreading, low-growing evergreen fern with leathery, pinnate leaves. It is one of the hardiest species and is especially suited for gardens with lime-free soil.

The Shield Fern *(Polystichum lobatum)* reaches a height of about 15 inches (60 cm.) and has rigid, leathery, evergreen leaves with glossy upper surfaces. It is a native of the mountain woodlands.

An eminently suitable fern for rocky lay-outs is the fresh, evergreeen Common Spleenwort *(Asplenium trichomanes)* with reddish brown leaf-stalks and narrow, finely cut fronds. It reaches a height of only 7 to 10 inches (15 to 20 cm.) and grows on rocks, tree stumps and in old walls in the shade. In the wild it is found at elevations of up to 9,000 to 12,000 feet (3,000 to 4,000 metres). Closely resembling this species is the somewhat smaller *Asplenium viride* with soft, green ribs that are brown only on the underside.

The smallest fern in cultivation is the Wall Rue *(Asplenium ruta-muraria)*. It is tiny, $1\frac{1}{2}$ to 6 inches (3 to 15 cm.) high, and grows abundantly on rocks and old walls. Surprisingly enough it tolerates sun quite well and even occasional dry spells. It is an excellent base for certain flowering rock plants, e.g. the Mountain Bell Flowers *(Campanula)*.

Another unusual fern is the Hard Fern *(Blechnum spicant)*. It, too, is an evergreen species, distinguished by differing fertile and sterile leaves, the former being taller, erect and with narrower forks. Mature plants grow to a height of about 12 inches (30 cm.) and prefer moist, peaty, forest soils without lime. They like a damper situation than most other ferns and appreciate an acid soil and light shade.

Very popular with rock gardeners is the pretty

Scale Fern *(Ceterach officinarum)* 4 to 8 inches (10 to 20 cm.) high. This evergreen fern makes clumps of short-ribbed, leathery, simple pinnate leaves and is found in the wild even on absolutely dry rocks and walls. It is eminently suitable for rock crevices and is very long-lived when once it takes hold. The Scale Fern does well in both sun and partial shade and requires a light protective covering of fir branches or bracken in winter.

As a rule ferns are not fastidious plants but they do not tolerate loss of root-stock and some species also loss of leaves. This must always be kept in mind, especially when propagating by division. They like forest soil with pine needles, moss and leaves, in other words humus-type soil, even stony soil, but always with good drainage and sufficient moisture.

Ferns are planted according to size, specific character and shape in the shaded parts of the garden and rock garden where, if carefully selected, they can be combined with certain flowering perennials. Small usually evergreen species are effective with Snowdrop Anemone *(Anemone silvestris)*, Primulas, Navelwort *(Omphalodes verna)* and also Barrenwort *(Epimedium)*. Taller species are effective planted with Foxglove *(Digitalis)*, tall Bell Flowers *(Campanula latifolia* and *Campanula persicifolia)*, Snake Root *(Cimicifuga)*, Goat's Beard *(Aruncus)* and Common Woodruff *(Asperula odorata)*.

# Hardy Ornamental Grasses

It is not so long ago that ornamental grasses began to be planted in gardens and rock gardens in greater number. Their wider use in various parts of the garden was hampered by insufficient knowledge of the requirements of different species and by the mistaken notion that grass is plentiful and that therefore it is unnecessary to grow it in the garden. Suitably selected grasses, however, can greatly enhance the beauty and give a more natural aspect to the various parts of the garden and their elegance, growth and colouration make them just as much of an ornament as many a flowering perennial.

Grasses are especially important in thin plantings of perennials in rock gardens, heath gardens, lakes and their immediate vicinity, bog gardens, and even in natural, only partially cultivated gardens where they rank among the very useful and undemanding plants. Grasses lighten the formal effect of perennial beds, thus heightening the impact of the individual species and the beauty of their flowers.

Low grasses are grown in rock gardens as well as on large areas in the sun and partial shade, serving as a ground cover between the various perennials. Many grasses provide neighbouring plants with a welcome winter cover and also natural humus. Some prefer dry, sunny banks which they strengthen with their roots, whereas others, of forest origin, like shade and still others even very damp situations.

If we wish to plant a small alpine meadow with several delicate plants, which even in gardens have a very moderate growth, together with alpine grasses we must not forget that the latter do not retain the low height of their original alpine habitat. It is therefore necessary to select species whose growth can be controlled. However, even the true grasses offer a choice of small species such as the blue-green to yellow-green *Festuca glacialis* making flat, compact tufts, or *Festuca punctoria*, a prickly, blue-green species from Asia Minor which is particularly well suited for the smaller rock garden. The somewhat taller, blue-grey *Festuca glauca*, up to 8 inches (20 cm.) high, is excellent in mass plantings in the sun. The rich green *Festuca scoparia* of the Pyrenees is very effective between small woody plants.

Further interesting *Festuca* grasses include the blue-green *Festuca amethystina*, up to 12 inches (30 cm.) high, and its somewhat smaller garden form 'April green', coloured a fresh grey-green, as well as *Festuca gigantea*, making huge, 20 to 30 inches (50 to 80 cm.) high clumps with pendant leaves, and the small, blue-green *Festuca vallesiaca* 'Glaucantha' only about 4 inches (10 cm.) high. To retain their attractive appearance and colour these grasses should be planted in poor, dry turf soil mixed with sand. All ornamental grasses provide good ground cover, prevent drying of the soil and are firm and persistent, spread easily and never become weeds.

# Heathers

Heathers are late summer flowering plants. In the wild they are usually found on heaths, moorlands and also on hillsides in Scotland and Wales, where they often cover large areas. Sometimes they make small compact tufts whereas at other times, especially on good soils, they attain a height of 3 feet (1 metre). Parts of clearings shaded by the surrounding trees are completely devoid of heather.

In the garden the best place for heathers and other heath plants is the heath garden, which may be located at the foot of the rock garden, on a slope or on level ground. It can also be laid out elsewhere, for example beneath tall trees. A natural aspect is provided by several large, weathered boulders placed at random. Very effective in the heath garden itself and in its immediate vicinity are several randomly planted conifers, best of all the tall growing, dwarf Juniper *(Juniperus communis* 'Hibernica'), *Rhododendron*, *Cotoneaster* which has a crop of red berries in the autumn, Brooms *(Genista* and *Cytisus)*; all brighten these parts of the garden with a profusion of striking blossoms from spring till early summer.

The most important plants in the heath garden, of course, are the heathers. The edges can be planted with smaller groups of quite low-growing heathers such as the Common Ling *(Calluna vulgaris* 'Foxii'), only 6 inches (15 cm.) high, dark greeen with small rose-violet flowers, or *Calluna vulgaris* 'Nana', also a dwarf species with small, purplish-red flowers. These forms do not bear many blossoms, as a rule, but they make nice, low carpets of fresh green.

Horticultural establishments offer a great number of beautiful garden forms, a few of the most distinct being *Calluna vulgaris* 'Alba Plena' — white, fine double, 12 to 16 inches (30 to 40 cm.) high, 'Alportii' — erect with glowing dark-red flowers, 'Flore Pleno' — long-flowering with a profusion of double pink blossoms, 'County Wicklow' — small, compact, bright pink, 'H. E. Beale' — a very good taller variety bearing a wealth of double pink flowers with white centres in September and October, 'Mullion' — a small variety, suitable as ground cover for larger areas, and 'Tib' with a wealth of double pink-red flowers. One of the smallest heathers is 'Sister Ann' with interesting grey-green foliage and small violet-pink flowers.

Heathers flower from July until October depending on the species and besides the attractiveness of their flowers they also provide abundant food for bees. They do well in every good lime-free, light, humus-type and sandy garden soil with peat, best of all in the sun.

No heath garden should be without the spring, summer and autumn heathers of the genus *Erica*. The spring flowering, from December to April, *Erica carnea* does well even in soil with some lime. Summer flowering species include, for example, several varieties of the Common Heather *(Erica cinerea)*, such as 'Atropurpurea', which attains a height of about 8 inches (20 cm.) and bears lovely dark red flowers from June till September, the 6 to 8 inches (15 to 20 cm.) high, carmine 'C. G. Best' and the 6 to 8 inches

(15 to 20 cm.) high, bright pink 'Rosea Splendens'.

Of the so-called autumn heathers, flowering from late summer until autumn, worthy of note are the small compact ones whose bright coloured blossoms are especially welcome at this time of year. These include, for instance, the 8 to 10 inches (20 to 25 cm.) white Cornish Heath *(Erica vagans* 'Alba'*)*, the early, white 'Lyonesse' flowering already in May, the 8 to 10 inch (20 to 25 cm.) high 'Mrs. D. F. Maxwell' bearing thick clusters of bright, salmon-red flowers, the 8 to 10 inches (20 to 25 cm.) salmon-pink 'St. Keverne' and the rose-red 'Rubra'.

Besides the previously mentioned heathers there are a number of other species, varieties and forms that can be successfully grown in the heath garden. These include several important genera from the family of heath plants, Ericaceae e.g. the Bog Rosemary *(Andromeda polifolia)* with the two dwarf forms 'Compacta' and 'Minima' which have pink, urn-shaped flowers and narrow, grey-green leaves; the Spice Heath *(Bruckenthalia spiculifolia)* with pinkish red flowers; St. Daboec's Heath *(Daboecia cantabrica)* with red, pendant, egg-shaped blossoms, glistening white in the form 'Alba', appearing from June until October or November, the undemanding evergreen Crowberry *(Empetrum nigrum)* with tiny, purplish-pink flowers, and the Azure Sage *(Pernettya mucronata)*, also an evergreen, with interesting red, purple or white berries, available in several garden forms.

All these heath plants like lime-free, humus-type soil with added peat or leaf mould.

Semi-shaded parts of the heath garden can be planted with Azaleas and Rhododendrons. They, too, require a light, lime-free soil with peat and their early abundant flowers are welcome sights which greatly enhance the heath garden.

## Propagation of Rock Plants

Beginners generally want to have the greatest possible number of species it their rock garden, if only one specimen of each. In time, however, they discover that it is better and the effect is more harmonious if larger areas and whole spaces between stones are planted to only one species, variety or form. This arrangement is the one that will bring out the beauty of rock plants, especially with the so-called common species such as the prostrate Phloxes *(Phlox subulata)*, Purple Rock Cress *(Aubrieta)* and Rock Soapwort *(Saponaria ocymoides)*.

And this brings us to the propagation of rock plants; they can be propagated by seed, division, cuttings and some also by grafting, particularly the more precious species such as the Prickly Thrift *(Acantholimon)*.

One of the easiest and most natural means of propagation is by seed. The end of winter and very early spring is a good time for sowing most perennials, and thus also for most rock plants. The seeds, a large number if need be, should be sown into boxes, bowls or flowerpots put in a slightly heated or cold garden frame. Common hardy species can be sown directly in the bed. When sowing it is necessary to keep in mind the requirements of the individual species. A universal soil mixture that will do for most of the common species is a loose, ripe hothouse soil or garden soil plus sand, peat also leaf mould. If the seeds are sown into bowls, boxes or flowerpots it is necessary to provide them with good drainage. These vessels are then placed in a cold garden frame, but after first having let the seeds freeze in the case of winter and pre-spring sowing. This is especially important in the case of high alpine plants, for the freezing has a beneficial effect on germination, just as in the wild. When the first true leaves of the plant have developed, it can be pricked out either into troughs or transplanted directly into small flowerpots, of course into a soil mixture suitable for the particular species. Later the plants can be transferred into larger flowerpots or directly to the rockery or bed.

The common rock plants such as Mouse-ear Chickweeds *(Cerastium)*, Purple Rock Cress *(Aubrieta)*, Madwort *(Alyssum)* and similar undemanding plants can be sown later in spring, March to April, but not so late that they would not be well grown by autumn and would remain small throughout the winter, thus being exposed to the risk of being "pulled up" easily by the frost, after which they would dry up and die.

With certain rock plants, e.g. the Pasque Flower *(Pulsatilla)*, it is recommended to sow the seeds immediately on ripening, thus attaining much better results than if they were sown in early spring of the following year.

Some rock plants, provided conditions are favourable, make self-sown seedlings, e.g. Flax *(Linum)*,

Toadflax *(Linaria)*, *Erinus*, *Primula*, *Soldanella* and Violets *(Viola)*. This, as a rule, is welcomed by the gardener, but on the other hand they can also become unpleasant weeds, taking up space and food material, to the detriment of their more delicate neighbours.

The list of well known rock plants that can easily be grown from the seed includes also the Alpine or Himalayan Asters *(Aster alpinus, A. subcoeruleus* and *A. amellus)*, the Columbines *(Aquilegia)*, Bell Flowers *(Campanula)*, Pinks *(Dianthus)*, Anemones *(Anemone)*, *Bergenia*, Fumitory *(Corydalis)*, Whitlow Grass *(Draba)*, Avens *(Geum)*, Fleabane *(Erigeron)*, Lavender *(Lavandula)*, Edelweiss *(Leontopodium)*, Musk *(Mimulus)*, Evening Primrose *(Oenothera)*, Poppy *(Papaver)*, Soapwort *(Saponaria)*, Spiderwort *(Tradescantia)* and many others.

Some rock plants have a fairly long period of germination, some have poor germination, also seedlings sometimes flower only after two or three years and some are too variable. For these reasons it is necessary to consider whether it would be better to select some other method of propagation.

Bulbs can also be propagated from the seed but this is a lengthy process and therefore it is better to separate the bulblets which grow around the parent bulb, after flowering and plant them in the autumn.

One of the commonest forms of propagation is by division of large clumps. This not only provides a great number of new individuals with exactly the same characteristics as the parent plant but also regenerates old and weakened plants, after being transferred to fresh soil they are much more vigorous and produce a profusion of lovely flowers. Rock plants can be divided both in the spring and autumn, the best time is, however, after flowering. In the case of autumn division, care should be taken that the plants have time to become well rooted before the onset of winter. This method can be used for a great number of well known rock plants, Primulas, Phloxes, Stonecrop *(Sedum)*, Gentians *(Gentiana acaulis)*, Rockfoil *(Saxifraga)*, Asters *(Aster dumosus)* as well as ornamental grasses and many other plants.

Some plants are propagated also by runners or rhizomes, which are simply detached from the plant and planted out directly into the bed or rockery. This method is used primarily for Irises *(Iris)*, Violet *(Viola odorata)*, Mouse-ear Chickweeds *(Cerastium)*, prostrate Phlox *(Phlox subulata)*, Periwinkle *(Vinca minor)*, certain Anemones such as *Anemone silvestris*, as well as for Snake Root *(Asarum)*, Rock Jasmine *(Androsace)*, New Zealand Bur *(Acaena)* and other similar plants.

A further means of propagation by taking cuttings, is used mainly for certain woody plants, but also for many rock plants such as Thyme *(Thymus)*, Stonecrop *(Sedum)*, prostrate Phlox *(Phlox subulata)*, hardy Prickly Pears *(Opuntia)*, Candytuft *(Iberis)*, Rock Cress *(Arabis)* and Sun Rose *(Helianthemum)*. These are hardy plants which take root fairly easily throughout the entire growing season. Cuttings should be put in a mixture of sandy soil, peat and well rotted humus, either directly in the selected spot or, in the case of rock or woody plants that do not strike so well, in a trough or frame covered with glass. By using growth hormone powders cuttings will strike far sooner and more reliably, even in such species which normally do not take roots readily, e.g. certain conifers.

Yet another and comparatively easy method of propagation is by layering — this consists of inserting branches into humus rich soil and pegging them there until they have made good roots; they are then detached from the parent plant. This method is suitable for Thyme *(Thymus)*, Pinks *(Dianthus)*, Periwinkle *(Vinca minor)* and above all for many species of shrubs, chiefly *Daphne cneorum*, *D. arbuscula* and *D. blagayana*, heathers, Spice Heath *(Bruckenthalia)* and other ericaceous plants.

## Small Bulbous and Tuberous Plants

Bulbous plants are true heralds of spring. Besides the well known Snowdrop *(Galanthus)*, Snowflake *(Leucojum)*, Grape Hyacinth *(Muscari)* and Bluebell *(Scilla)*, this group includes a wide range of other bulbs as well as certain low-growing tuberous plants such as the winter Aconite *(Eranthis)*, Anemones *(Anemone)* etc. whose lovely flowers enhance the beauty of the garden, in spring.

Small bulbous and tuberous plants are eminently suited for borders and beds or as an underplanting and complement to ornamental shrubs, freely planted in the grass or in the woodland garden and naturally also in the rock garden where their low growth and early flowering is of particular advantage.

The chief condition of success in growing bulbs is

a well prepared but not freshly fertilized loamy-sandy soil, that is not too damp and above all not permanently damp. It is also important to plant bulbs at the correct time and at the required depth. They do not tolerate fresh manure or compost or nitrogen fertilizers. However, they appreciate an annual surface manuring of well rotted compost, before the onset of winter. In autumn planting it may easily happen that the plant does not grow good roots and therefore has poor-growth and flowering in the spring. The correct depth for planting is three times the size of the bulb, in other words in the case of Scillas *(Scilla)* or Crocus about 2 to 3 inches (5 to 8 cm.). Cultivated as well as the so-called botanical Tulips are planted 4 inches (10 to 12 cm.) and large Narcissi not less than 6 inches (15 cm.) below the surface. Tulip bulbs should be spaced about 5 inches (12 cm.) apart, Narcissi are better planted in groups in partial shade and other small bulbous plants also in groups about 2 to 3 inches (5 to 6 cm.) apart. These spring flowering bulbs are not intolerant of a light covering of carpeting plants in the rock garden.

Bulbs can be planted from about mid-August to October; species grown in flowerpots may be planted even in spring or at any time during the growing period. Most bulbs tolerate even severe frosts. Only in situations where the soil is too damp do they tend to be less hardy and often rot.

All small bulbous and tuberous plants are very good companions. However, they should not be planted too close to vigorous perennials or large carpeting plants for they will not thrive as they should.

The range of bulbous and tuberous plants is very wide and therefore we will only mention those that are best suited for the rock garden.

*Allium* includes not only useful plants such as onion, garlic, leek and chive, but also many lovely ornamental species that are welcome additions to the spring and summer garden. The commonest species are the yellow Garlic *(Allium moly)* and the carmine-pink *Allium ostrowskianum;* both flower in June. *Allium karatawiense*, an April flowerer, has lilac-pink flowers and decorative broad leaves and *Allium narcissiflorum* from the Alps has lovely pink blossoms.

Some of the tuberous Anemones worthy of note are the variable Poppy Anemones *(Anemone coronaria)* cultivated in several garden forms, single as well as double, and in a number of shades. They grow comparatively well, but in the dormant period they often suffer from excess moisture. The dark blue *Anemone apenina* and the various forms of *Anemone blanda* are well suited for the rockery and woodland garden.

Glory of the Snow *(Chionodoxa)* is distinguished by an exceptionally profuse flowering. It does best in lightly shaded, not too dry situations, where it spreads freely. It is easily propagated by seeds also; the flowers appear after two to three years.

Crocuses *(Crocus)* comprise many species, varieties and forms. They are divided into spring and autumn flowering species, the large-flowered species which are the ones usually found in gardens, and botanical species suitable for the garden and rock garden, as well as for free planting in woodland gardens and parks where they soon cover large areas. Crocuses are perennials, they spread quickly and flower profusely.

Aconites *(Eranthis)* decorate the garden and rockery from earliest spring with their golden flowers and if conditions are suitable sow themselves and spread freely.

The so-called bulbous Irises are referred to elsewhere. The beauty of their flowers makes them well deserving of a place in our gardens.

Worthy of particular note in the group of bulbous plants are the so-called botanical Tulips. One of the earliest flowerers is the Water-lily Tulip *(Tulipa kaufmanniana)*, small, originally yellowish-white, but today in many colour varieties thanks to selection and hybridisation. Perhaps the most spectacular of all are the tulips of the group Fosteriana, the finest and best known being 'Madame Lefeber', a magnificent red tulip with a yellow-black-rimmed star inside the blossom. *Tulipa tarda*, chief representative of the many-flowered tulips, is described next to the illustration.

Also included in this group of bulbous plants are the dwarf Daffodils of the *bulbocodium* group of species. Besides the type, the Hoop Petticoat Daffodil *(Narcissus bulbocodium)*, there are many interesting varieties and subvarieties in cultivation bearing flowers in various shades of yellow. *Narcissus nanus* and its garden form 'Little Beauty' are also eminently suitable for the rock garden.

# Trees and Shrubs for the Rock Garden and Its Immediate Vicinity

If a rock garden is to look natural it must be incorporated into and harmonize with the garden as a whole. This is partially achieved by planting individuals or groups of ornamental shrubs, small deciduous trees and conifers. It is best to select natural shapes and foliage of unobtrusive colouration so as not to disrupt the natural effect of the rockery.

The selection of ornamental trees and shrubs is determined not only by the taste of the grower but also by the size of the rockery and entire garden as well as by the purpose they are to serve. Last, but not least, it is also necessary to take into consideration the position and the soil, for these plants are generally intended to remain in the selected spot for a long time.

The selection of ornamental shrubs and conifers is limited to those that do not have a too heavy or too vigorous growth. These are then distributed about the site. Some can be concentrated say, in the heath garden, where it is also possible to include several more pretentious woody plants such as the dwarf Japanese Maple *(Acer palmatum)*, dwarf Birch *(Betula nana)* and a wide range of ericaceous plants, including Azaleas and Rhododendrons, chiefly the low-growing botanical species.

In the rock garden and round the edges we can also plant certain smaller Barberries such as *Berberis thunbergii* and the deciduous variety 'Atropurpurea', and even the red-leaved dwarf form 'Atropurpurea Nana' which attain a height of about 18 inches

(40 cm.). *B. verruculosa* is a small evergreen shrub about 3 feet (1 metre) high with comparatively large, golden-yellow flowers. Also suitable are evergreen as well as deciduous *Cotoneaster* species of various heights and forms. The Japanese Quince *(Chaenomeles japonica)*, *Daphne mezereum*, *Cytisus*, *Genista* and many other shrubs and shrublets are excellent for the rock garden and its immediate vicinity.

Particularly attractive when in bloom in early spring are the Daphnes, especially if they are planted in groups. Of the low-growing species worthy of particular note are the evergreen *Daphne cneorum*, which fills the rockery with a flood of pink blossoms and a powerful scent during May and the pink-violet flowered *Daphne arbuscula*, which is a lovely sight at all times of the year and is easy to grow.

Very effective in the rock garden are the bright red berries of the Spindle Tree *(Euonymus)*, St. John's Wort *(Hypericum calycinum)* bears golden-yellow blooms, and Cinquefoil *(Potentilla fruticosa)* in several yellow or white forms flower during the summer.

Near the rock garden we can plant the evergreen Holly *(Ilex)*, and of the larger shrubs the white *Magnolia stellata* or some of the dwarf species or forms of Mock Orange *(Philadelphus)* or the evergreen Firethorn *(Pyracantha)* with its attractive red-orange berries in the autumn. The rock garden can also include the dwarf Willow *(Salix)* or one of the smaller *Spiraea* shrubs. The wonderful fragrant Snowball Tree *(Viburnum carlesii)* as well as the more recent hybrid *V. carlcephalum*, which are related to the honeysuckle, are gaining in popularity amongst gardeners.

The basic and predominant colour of conifers must always be a rich green, albeit in various differing shades, for the framework of the natural rock garden must not be more decorative than the rockery itself. Some of the most natural and thus most attractive conifers for larger rock gardens and their immediate vicinity includes the Mountain Pine *(Pinus montana)*; well suited for the smaller rock garden is the smaller variety *Pinus montana pumilio* and as a backdrop the noble Arolla Pine *(Pinus cembra)*, possibly also other slow-growing pines could be planted. In the rock garden itself it is possible to plant a great number of dwarf, often exotic-looking conifers, for example Spruces *(Picea)*, Cypress *(Chamaecyparis)* and the Abor-vitae *(Thuja)*. Golden or grey-blue conifers are effective only if set in a carpet of fresh green and if they are not too many. Popular for planting in the natural rock gardens is the slender, silvery Juniper *(Juniperus communis* 'Hibernica'*)*; in larger rock gardens, e.g. in the heath garden, they can be more freely planted. Other attractive trees besides dwarf Cypress are the low, prostrate *Junipers* such as *J. horizontalis*, *J. sabina*, *J. squamata* 'Meyeri' or dwarf Spruces such as the slow-growing *Picea glauca* 'Conica'. Also well suited are the broadly nest-shaped Spruces, not only for the rock garden and in grass, but also on banks where, however, it is necessary to provide them with water in dry periods.

Some conifers are distinguished by a lovely spherical shape, e.g. the Eastern Arbor-vitae *(Thuja occidentalis* 'Globosa' and *T. occidentalis* 'Recurva Nana').

Conifers should be transplanted in spring and in the

autumn. When set out they should not be cut back and appreciate not very frequent but thorough waterings after planting; in very dry and windy weather occasional spraying is better than continual watering. Neither natural manure nor artifical fertilizers should be applied when planting; all that is necessary is loose topsoil with old, well-rotted compost.

# PLATES

# Prickly Thrift    Plumbaginaceae

*Acantholimon glumaceum*

Prickly Thrift is a hardy, low growing evergreen plant which forms firm cushions bearing spikelets of carmine-pink flowers on short stems.

For cultivation *A. glumaceum* is one of the most rewarding of the approximately 80 species that grow wild on the steppes and mountains of eastern Europe and Asia Minor. It is tolerant of sun and does best in sheltered deep rock crevices or stony limestone outcrops in porous turf soil, mixed with sand and some limestone chips, in other words on a slope or in soil with good drainage where excess water quickly recedes or flows off. All species of *Acantholimon* are thermophilic and it is therefore recommended, especially in colder climates, to cover them with a light layer of fir branches or bracken before the onset of winter.

Under favourable conditions Prickly Thrift forms large cushions, attaining a height of about 6 inches (15 cm.) during the flowering period in July and August.

*A. glumaceum* can be propagated either from the seed or from lengthier hardwood cuttings which should be planted in August or September. These should be inserted fairly deep, watered with care and covered with glass in winter; the best method is to place in a cold garden frame and partially cover with light soil. The following spring the branches send out roots and are then separated from the parent plant and placed in porous soil in small flowerpots. Suitable companion plants are xerophilous high mountain alpines.

# Milfoil, Yarrow  Compositae
*Achillea tomentosa*

A popular rock garden plant forming a thick, silver-green growth. The golden yellow, many-flowered clusters are borne on 6 to 8 inches (15 to 20 cm.) high stalks. It grows wild on the dry slopes of southern Europe and its range extends to western Siberia.

*A. aurea* is a yellow flowering species only 6 inches (15 cm.) high, which is particularly attractive set next to the carmine-red alpine *Dianthus gratianopolitanus* and red *Dianthus deltoides* 'Splendens'. This species, flowering in June to August, prefers a dry site and light, porous soil. Only light watering is required in hot summer weather, to prevent excessive moist heat.

Of the white-flowering species one that is commonly cultivated is the silvery-leaved *A. clavennae* which forms cushions of delicately cut leaves and bears flowers 6 to 8 inches (15 to 20 cm.) high. It is a native of the southern slopes of the Alps and does well in dry, stony soil with good drainage. Other similar species are, *A. ageratifolia. A. kolbiana* and *A. serbica* which as a rule flower in early summer. White-leaved Milfoils are effective beside Prickly Thrift *(Acantholimon glumaceum)*, Speedwell *(Veronica rupestris)*, Soapwort *(Saponaria ocymoides)* and Sun Rose *(Helianthemum)* with green leaves.

All alpine Milfoils do well on dry walls and screes in the sun. They require a ripe soil, lightened with sand.

Propagation is by division of older clumps and by cuttings in spring and summer.

# Lebanon Candytuft, Store Cress

Cruciferae

*Aethionema warleyense*

The 40 species of this genus are hardy perennial small plants, suitable for rock gardens in full sun and rocky, calcareous soils. As a rule the leaves are small, blue-green to grey, and the flowers pink to purplish-red, sometimes even white, growing in clusters. These species are mostly natives of the Near East.

The largest of the genus is *A. grandiflorum*, covered with clusters of pink flowers, which does very well in rock crevices and dry walls. It attains a height of 12 inches (30 cm.) and forms loose bushes clothed with short, thick clusters of flowers appearing in May till July.

The loveliest of the genus, especially for the colour of the flowers and compact growth, is *A. warleyense*. Particularly attractive are the forms 'Warley Rose' with deep pink flowers and 'Warley Ruber' with dark red blooms. They flower in June. These plants are extremely well suited for planting in rock crevices and dry walls in the sun and also in screes in the rock garden. They like hot, sunny and comparatively dry situations and sandy-loamy soil. They do not tolerate damp, especially in winter.

Propagation is from the seed or by cuttings which should be taken in July. Division and transplanting of older plants is generally not successful.

It can be planted next to *Anacyclus*, Thrift *(Armeria caespitosa)* Whitlow Grass *(Draba)*, Madwort *(Alyssum spinosum)*, Houseleek *(Sempervivum)*, and Candytuft *(Iberis sempervirens)*.

# Flowering onion  Liliaceae

*Allium ostrowskianum*

This bulbous plant from Turkestan is grown in rock gardens chiefly for its bright pink-carmine, globose inflorescence about 9 inches (20 to 25 cm.) high. The flowers appear in June. One of the best of the genus is *A. narcissiflorum* (syn. *A. pedemontanum*) with large, nicely shaped, bright rose flowers, about 6 to 8 inches (15 to 20 cm.) high, appearing in June to July. This bulb is a native of the southern littoral limestone Alps where it grows in light, porous soil in warm, sunny situations.

The Golden Garlic *(A. moly)* of southern Europe is the prettiest of the yellow species. Attaining a height of as much as 12 inches (30 cm.) it has broadly lanceolate leaves and like all the plants of this genus is most effective in large groups. Of interest is the fact that this species has been grown in gardens since the 16th century.

Extraordinarily persistent is *A. cyaneum*, a native of west China, where it attains a height of about 8 inches (20 cm.) and bears blue flowers in July and August.

All the above named species grace the rock garden with their flowers in early summer. All look well in the natural rock garden amidst prairie plants, thermophilic grasses and in heath gardens.

Propagation is very easy by seed or by offsets; in suitable sites the plants reproduce themselves. The bulbs are planted 4 to 6 inches (10 to 15 cm.) deep according to the size of the bulbs and the type of soil, which should be loamy, sandy.

# Gold Dust  Cruciferae
*Alyssum saxatile*

Alyssums grow on low, limestone slopes and cliffs and are very popular spring rock plants. *A. saxatile* has grey-green leaves and bears a wealth of golden yellow flowers in early spring. This species has several attractive varieties such as *A. saxatile* 'Compactum' — only 4 to 6 inches (12 to 15 cm.) high and close growing, and *A. saxatile citrinum* with lemon yellow flowers. *A. saxatile* 'Flore Pleno' has a slower growth but has more abundant and longer-lasting flowers than the other varieties. Interesting for its bright foliage is *A. saxatile* 'Variegatum', also characterized by slower growth. The last two varieties can be propagated only by vegetative means, by cuttings after the termination of the flowering period.

Alyssums are best in dry walls, fissures, edgings, rock gardens and slopes in the sun. All are noted for their wealth of flowers — *A. saxatile* and its varieties in May and the prostrate Alyssums in May and June.

Good companions are the blue and violet *Aubrieta, Arabis, Phlox subulata, Saponaria ocymoides,* etc.

Older Alyssums should not be transplanted and it is recommended to top dress them with loose loamy-sandy soil after the termination of flowering.

Propagation is by seed or taking cuttings in June. The seed should be sown in spring and it usually germinates after two weeks.

## *Anacyclus depressus*                          Compositae

This plant is the only one of 15 species native to the Mediterranean region, mainly found in the hills of Morocco, that is cultivated in our rock gardens. It makes prostrate rosettes of silver-green, finely-cut foliage closely pressed to the ground, and bears a large number of white flowers in May and June that open only in sunny weather. The backs of the flowers are carmine and particularly attractive are the closed red buds, opening during the day into white blossoms. *A. depressus* attains a height of 2 to 4 inches (5 to 10 cm.), depending on the soil.

Good location of these plants is very important. They do well in spaces between rocks, in rock fissures as well as in the joins of dry walls. The soil should be sandy, dry, porous, lime-free and poor in humus.

Excessive moisture in summer is harmful to the plant, the same being true of damp in winter. The former is avoided by planting in porous soil with good drainage and winter damp is prevented by covering with fir branches or bracken.

Propagation is easy from the seed, which is sown in a box and kept through the winter months in a cold frame. The seedlings are first pricked out into pots and after they have rooted well are planted out in the open. Older plants cannot be transferred without risk.

This species should be interplanted with Lebanon Candytuft *(Aethionema)*, Pasque Flower *(Pulsatilla)*, St. John's Wort *(Hypericum polyphyllum)*, *Festuca* grasses and also certain species of Cinquefoil *(Potentilla)*.

## Rock Jasmine     Primulacaeae
*Androsace chamaejasme*

## Sea Heath     Frankeniaceae
*Frankenia laevis*

Androsaces are plants from high altitudes, those in cultivation are natives of the European and Asian mountains.

Preference is given to the Asiatic species for they do better in cultivation. These include *A. mucronifolia* which makes 2 to 4 inches (5 to 10 cm.) high clumps of rosettes with small green leaves enveloped with cluster of pink flowers.

The limestone rocks of the Jura and Tatra Mountains are the home of *A. lactea*. The rosettes of narrow green leaves bear milky-white flowers with a yellow eye. This plant requires partial shade, humus rich soil and good drainage.

*A. chamaejasme* is an attractive, high alpine plant making clumps of hairy rosettes reaching a height of only 2 to 3 inches (5 to 8 cm.). The flowers, white with yellow eye, turn pink with a red eye on aging and appear from June to July. The conditions for good growth are the same as for *A. lactea*.

Propagation is by division of the easy-growing rosettes and by seed.

*Frankenia laevis* is a native evergreen, prostrate plant, forming mats of small grey-green leaves. The thick growth is about 2 to 3 inches (5 to 10 cm.) high and bears a profusion of flowers in June to July. These are practically sessile and an attractive rose-pink. In cultivation this species is especially well suited as a cover plant with bulbs or for growing in paved path crevices. It prefers dry, porous and sandy soil and full sun. Rather sensitive to winter cold it should be covered with fir branches or bracken.

# Japanese Anemone  Ranunculaceae
*Anemone japonica*

Autumn Anemones are natives of the Far East. The most important of these is *A. japonica* which is found growing in the semi-shady mountain forests of central China in an almost subtropical climate. The plants, which attain a height of 2 to 3 feet (60 to 100 cm.), have bright green, tripartite, trilobed leaves. From August on, sometimes till the first frost, the plant is covered with a profusion of delicately coloured flowers resembling large wild roses with golden anthers. Of the better known forms the ones most frequently cultivated are the garden forms 'Honorine Joubert' — single, snow-white, 'Queen Charlotte' — semi-double, pink tinged with violet and 'Prince Henry' — semi-double, red.

Closely resembling *A. japonica* is *A. vitifolia*, native of the western Himalayas, which has a fairly vigorous growth and bears a large number of white to pinkish flowers. It is very resistant, in fact practically indestructible. It does well both in a sunny position and in semi-shade and flowers from summer till late autumn.

All Anemones do well in ripe, garden soil, leaf mould and sand. Too dry soil should be avoided and permanent damp is also harmful. They have little resistance to frost and should therefore be well covered with a layer of leaves.

*A. japonica* is propagated by root cuttings taken in spring or autumn, *A. vitifolia* by seed. The best time for transplanting is in spring.

If set out as solitary plants it is recommended to place them with Monkshood *(Aconitum)*, hardy ferns, Foam flower *(Tiarella)*, Ragwort *(Senecio przewalski)* and similar vigorous perennials.

## Snowdrop Anemone — Ranunculaceae
*Anemone silvestris* 'Grandiflora'

The type plant *Anemone silvestris* has a wide distribution from south-west Europe to eastern Siberia. It attains a height of 10 to 16 inches (25 to 40 cm.) and bears slightly pendant, pure white flowers in late spring. The olive-green foliage is also very decorative.

Most commonly found in gardens, sparsely wooded grounds, and large, slightly shaded rock gardens is the large flowered variety *A. silvestris* 'Grandiflora', most effective when planted in large numbers, and the double variety *A. silvestris* 'Flore Pleno', formerly listed under the name 'Elise Fellmann'.

Also belonging to the group of spring flowerers is the Wood Anemone *(A. nemorosa)*, often found in deciduous and mixed woods in almost the whole of Europe, except for the southern regions, all the way to the Caucasus. The slender stems bear a single white flower tinged rose on the outside and resembling a wild rose.

The Yellow Wood Anemone *(A. ranunculoides)* is a much rarer plant in the wild, with dark yellow flowers, which looks well beside the White Wood Anemone *(A. nemorosa)*. It reaches a height of about 8 inches (20 cm.) and flowers in April to May.

All the above named species do very well in the woodland garden and rockery where the garden cultivated forms and varieties prove particularly effective.

In general they do well in loose, humus rich slightly limy soil.

Propagation is by seed, which must be harvested in time before it is dispersed, or by division of rootstock.

# Columbine — Ranunculaceae

*Aquilegia discolor*

*Aquilegia discolor* is a dainty species only 4 to 6 inches (10 to 15 cm.) high, a native of the Pyrenees. It is most effective when correctly placed in the rock garden, either in not too large rock crevices or at the base of the rockery. It bears delicate blue flowers in late spring.

In the wild some Columbines are to be found growing just below the tree line, e.g. the high alpine *A. alpina* 12 to 16 inches (30 to 40 cm.) high and bearing solitary, bright blue flowers. These, however, are only rarely found at the nurseryman's.

*A. einseleana*, a native of the southern Alps, attains a height of 6 to 10 inches (15 to 25 cm.) and has delicate foliage; the blue-violet flowers appear in June and July. It grows on the rocky slopes of limestone formations at elevations up to 5,400 feet (1,800 metres). *A. flabellata* 'Alba Nana', a native of Japan, is a striking and frequently cultivated species attaining a height of up to 10 inches (25 cm.). It has white flowers, appearing in June and July, and grey-green foliage.

Low-growing Columbines prefer loose, humus rich soil and sunny, though not very hot, or slightly shaded situations.

Propagation is by seed sown in boxes; the seedlings are pricked out into small flowerpots and after they have taken root are planted out in the open. American and Japanese species require a light cover in winter.

These plants are effective amidst *Potentilla argyrophylla*, *Geum montanum*, *Anemone silvestris* 'Grandiflora' *Eriophyllum umbellatum* and *Eriophyllum caespitosum* (syn. *Bahia lanata*).

# Rock Cress     Cruciferae

*Arabis albida*

Flowering in early spring, these plants have been cultivated a long time and include several much-valued garden forms, e.g. from the Caucasian species *A. albida* (syn. *A. alpina* and *A. caucasica*), 4 to 8 inches (10 to 20 cm.) high. These are the large-flowered *A. albida* 'Grandiflora', *A. albida* 'Schneehaube' with tall clusters of pure white flowers, the pale sulphur yellow *A. albida* 'Sulphurea', the pink *A. albida* 'Rosea, *A. albida* 'Variegata' with white flowers and yellow leaves, and *A. albida* 'Pleniflora' with double white flowers resembling those of the Lilies-of-the-Valley. All these garden varieties are excellent in the rock garden, in borders and flower beds, and also in the cemetery on graves. Lower forms are also planted on dry walls.

The crossing of *A. aubrietioides* x *A. caucasica* produced the so-called *arendsii* forms of which the most interesting are the carmine pink var. *atropurpurea*, the pale to dark pink 'Rosabella' and the dark pink var. *coccinea*. All flower in April and May, have a lower growth and are welcome additions to the spring rock garden.

These smaller forms can be planted between *Draba olympica, Dianthus caesius, Androsace mucronifolia, Saxifraga apiculata*, etc. They do well in a sunny situation in limy, porous soil, preferably poorer so that the plants do not grow too vigorously and retain their true alpine form.

Propagation is by seed, division of older clumps and cuttings.

Taller forms can be planted with *Alyssum, Aubrieta, Aethionema, Phlox subulata*, and *Helianthemum*.

# Thrift, Sea Pink — Plumbaginaceae

*Armeria maritima*

Their bright colours in the spring as well as the ease of cultivation make Thrifts popular plants for the rock garden. Natives of south-western Europe, they found their way into gardens in about 1886. The plants generally form close-set cushions with even, spreading growth, making them a good substitute for turf. However, they can also be planted in borders, at the base of the rockery and as edgings for paths. In the wild, both on the seacoast and in the mountains, they grow in loose, sandy soil or fine screes in deep humus rich soil. They require a dry, sunny position.

The forms may be high or low and besides the main flowering period in spring, some bloom several times more up until autumn.

*A. maritima* the species most commonly found in cultivation, makes firm cushions up to 4 inches (10 cm.) high and bears pink-red flowers in May and June. This species has given rise to several pretty garden varieties, e.g. *A. maritima* 'Alba' with pure white flowers on stems 6 inches (15 cm.) long, *A. maritima* 'Laucheana Splendens' with longer stems and bright pink flowers, 'Crimson Gem' — dark red with thick foliage, 'Rosea Compacta' — carmine-pink, 'Solendens Perfecta' — bright red, with only 4 to 5 inch (10 to 12 cm.) long stems.

Taller Thrifts are propagated by seed or more commonly by division in spring or after flowering; seedlings, however, do not breed true.

Pinks *(Dianthus caesius, Dianthus deltoides)*, *Arabis*, *Aubrieta*, *Campanula*, *Draba dedeana* and similar plants are suitable companions.

# Wormwood                                    Compositae

*Artemisia lanata*

The plants of this genus have a widespread natural distribution in Europe, Asia and North America. They are to be found in the plains as well as high in the mountains on steep, inaccessible rocks in the sun. They have delicate, aromatic leaves, the mountain species tend to hug the ground, and all bear insignificant flowers.

Of the low-growing species, one of the most popular is *A. lanata* (syn. *A. pedemontana*) with silver-grey, pubescent leaves, attaining a height of no more than 1 to 2 inches (2 to 5 cm.).. A native of the southern Alps, it grows on limestone in a truly harsh environment of sun and drought. Therefore it is a xerophilous plant and watering is not recommended when growing in a rock garden, for then it generally dies. It should be planted in the rockery or a dry wall in the sun, where growth is rapid and thick cushions are soon formed. The yellow-white flowers are very small and it is best to cut them off. In the rock garden this species is grown only in dry situations, mainly for its lovely, silvery foliage.

Wormwoods are effective in rock gardens in rock fissures, on overhangs, walls and as a cover for the ground.

Their advantage lies in that they always remain fresh and attractive even in periods of drought.

The genus comprises about 200 species spread throughout most of the Northern Hemisphere. Some are ornamental, others are known for their medicinal properties or are used to flavour dessert wines and liqueurs.

# Alpine Aster                               Compositae
*Aster alpinus*

There are many species of Aster growing wild in Europe, Africa and America, some of these are cultivated, including *A. alpinus*. Besides the type species, there are also various natural varieties to be found in the wild. All these Asters are attractive and their profusion of flowers makes them an effective plant for garden beds, borders and especially steep rock-garden slopes. Suitable companion plants are the golden *Primula auricula*, azure-blue Gentian *(Gentiana clusii)*, yellow Milfoil *(Achillea tomentosa)*, the creeping Chalk Plant *(Gypsophila repens)*, delicate Bell Flower *(Campanula pusilla)* and other, generally hardy species.

*A. alpinus* has a natural distribution extending from the Alps and Carpathians across Persia to Siberia and grows at very high elevations, even above 9,000 feet (3,000 metres). As a rule, these plants do well in our gardens. They attain a height of 8 to 12 inches (20 to 30 cm.) during the flowering period and the blossoms decorate the garden with various shades of blue violet and pink as well as white in May and June.

The type plant, bearing lilac to rose-lilac flowers, has given rise to several garden varieties, e.g. *A. alpinus* 'Albus' with white flowers and *A. alpinus* 'Ruber' with rose-red blooms.

The easiest and most common method of propagation is by division after flowering i.e. in August, the stems being removed and the plant partially cut back. Propagation by seed is also possible, however, the seedlings do not come true.

# Michaelmas Daisy — Compositae

*Aster amellus*

This species occurs in the wild in various parts of Central Europe as well as in the Caucasus and western Asia. *A. amellus* belongs to a group of perennial species which have become great favourites for their profusion of bright flowers in late summer and early autumn.

In our gardens as well as in larger rock gardens one usually finds the cultivated forms. Well known and well worth growing are e.g. 'King George' — flowers dark violet, large, 16 inches (40 cm.) high, August-September, 'Gnom' — dark violet, 16 inches (40 cm.) high, September-October, 'Senia' — pale rose, somewhat taller up to 24 inches (60 cm.), August-September, and 'Hermann Löns' — large mauve-blue flowers, 24 inches (60 cm.) high with somewhat prostrate growth.

*A. amellus* likes sunny, dry situations, good garden soil that is porous and with some lime. In prolonged dry periods it welcomes occasional, but thorough waterings preferably at dusk. If left in one spot for several years, it will begin to lose its wealth of flowers and it is therefore necessary to divide the plants and transplant them.

It is best to plant *A. amellus* in borders and beds that are fairly spacious, where it is most effective in larger groups together with other perennials.

Propagation is possible by seed but the seedlings are unlikely to come true. All forms are propagated only by division of older clumps in the spring or autumn.

# Goat's Beard                                   Saxifragaceae
*Astilbe chinensis* 'Pumila'

This species is a dwarf perennial with attractive decorative foliage and deep red flowers clustered on a short spike. It attains a height of only 9 inches (20 to 25 cm.) and in July and August its inflorescence brightens the somewhat sparser flowers of the summer rock garden. It forms large colonies, especially on deep enough, humus rich soils in semi-shade.

Somewhat more demanding than the foregoing is *A. crispa*, a dwarf hybrid only 5 to 6 inches (12 to 15 cm.) high, with much cut leaves and pale rose flowers. *A. crispa* 'Perkeo' is a dwarf form only 6 inches (15 cm.) high, with purplish-lilac flowers.

Propagation is by seed or division, from spring till early May.

Good companions are Navelwort *(Omphalodes)*, *Waldsteinia*, *Moehringia* and similar plants.

Also popular perennials are the modern forms embracing a wide range of colours which are a must in the semi-shaded, moist parts of the garden. They are also effective on the edges of larger rock gardens and near water.

They like humus rich, fairly damp soil and even tolerate wet soil for a time. In adequately moist soil they do well also in the sun, otherwise in partial shade.

# Purple Rock Cress                        Cruciferae
*Aubrieta deltoidea*

This is a well known cushion plant, flowering profusely in the spring, and is a must for every garden. It is a native of Italy, the Balkans and Asia Minor. An extremely vigorous plant it forms small cushions soon after planting. It is put in rock gardens, dry walls as well as borders and likes a sunny, warm situation with loose, porous, nutritious and slightly limy soil. The plants should be cut back slightly after flowering, they should also be top dressed with light sandy soil and leaf mould.

After a mild winter, often as early as the beginning of April, the cushions are covered with a profusion of pale and dark blue flowers and more recent forms with red, white, violet and pink hues, thus creating a magnificent palette together with pink *Phlox sabulata*, white Candytuft *(Iberis)* and the golden Alyssum *(Alyssum saxatile)*.

Natural species are more ground hugging and sometimes also more resistant; the many cultivated varieties are somewhat taller and more colourful. *A. deltoidea* is the parent stock of all the forms sold by dealers as *Aubrieta* hybrids.

All attain a height of about 4 inches (10 cm.), and flower in April and May. In rock gardens they are most effective when planted in larger numbers resulting in sheets of magnificent colour.

Excessive sun, as well as too much moisture during their growth and propagation are detrimental.

## *Bergenia cordifolia*                               Saxifragaceae

These are rewarding plants with large round to ovate or oval, dark green, glossy, leathery leaves, attaining a height of 12 to 20 inches (30 to 50 cm.) during the flowering period. Evergreen, they make strong, creeping stems that send out new roots. The pink red, or white flowers are borne on thick stalks before the new leaves appear. The flowering period is in early spring, but there may be a second flowering in autumn.

Bergenias like a moist soil that does not dry out and a semi-shaded situation amidst trees, though they grow well in the sun. These almost indestructible plants can remain in one spot for years. However, from time to time it is necessary to cover the bared rootstock above the ground with good garden soil. Many dormant buds will come to life then and the plant will suddenly grow.

Only a few species are usually considered for cultivation in parks and gardens, the most common ones are *B. cordifolia*, a native of Siberia where it grows in sparse mountain forests, and *B. crassifolia*, a native of eastern Asia (Mongolia), which has a more compact growth and oval leaves measuring 8 to 12 inches (20 to 30 cm.). *B. cordifolia* is pale pink and *B. crassifolia* dark red to purple red, the flowers appearing very early, often in March. It is very good amidst or next to sparsely planted woody plants.

Propagation is by division or root cuttings in spring.

Good companions are various ferns, *Pachysandra*, *Sedum spectabile*, *Vinca minor*, Anemones *(Anemone silvestris)* and Lilies-of-the Valley *(Convallaria)*.

# Bell Flower  Campanulaceae

*Campanula bellidifolia*

Bell Flowers comprise a large group of plants with many species, varieties and forms, differing in growth, height, foliage, as well as shape and colour of the flowers and for that reason they are widely planted in gardens and rockeries. Some species are low, almost cushiony and are good in rock gardens, dry walls or borders, others are taller and are effective in larger beds amidst other perennials, also they are good as cut flowers or as solitary plants in turf.

The genus comprises about 200 species of which only a very few have a low or prostrate growth. It is these prostrate forms that are excellent for rock fissures, dry walls, in pavements and in crevices in the rock garden steps.

They tolerate semi-shade but flower much more profusely in sunny situations.

*C. bellidifolia*, shown here, is 1 to 5 inches (3 to 12 cm.) high and one of the rare Caucasian species. It has small dainty leaves resembling the Daisy (*Bellis* — hence the name) and forming small cushions from which the large, open, blue-violet bell-like flowers grow.

It requires porous soil, best of all turf soil with an addition of natural, ripe humus plus some brick rubble.

Propagation is by seed or division.

It can be planted next to *Dianthus*, *Gypsophila tenella*, *Hutchinsia*, *Iberis*, *Dryas*, *Ranunculus montanus* and a wide range of *Sedum*.

## *Campanula portenschlagiana*          Campanulaceae

The type plant *C. portenschlagiana* was introduced to garden cultivation as early as 1836. It is a mountain Bell Flower, a native of the Dalmatian coast of Yugoslavia and is one of the best for dry walls. It forms thick, evergreen mats about 4 inches (10 cm.) high, dotted in June and July with myriads of bright blue, open bells, arranged in clusters. This species grows best in sandy-rocky soil and is effective beside walls and on rock gardens. The main flowering is during the summer but there is a second one in the autumn.

A beautiful garden variety is called 'Birch', which has a more compact growth, and larger brighter coloured flowers. It attains a height of about 6 inches (15 cm.) and its second, autumn flowering is even more profuse than that of *C. portenschlagiana*.

Other forms in this group of creeping Bell Flowers, without any special requirements are the following subspecies from the southern Alps, Italy and Greece: *C. garganica* and its slightly smaller, natural subspecies *C. garganica fenestrelata* and *C. garganica istriaca*; they have low, bright green cushions which either grow in rock fissures, or hang down from the rocks and are dotted with small but lovely bells in early summer.

These Bell Flowers are generally propagated by division, but also by seed or by cuttings. Suitable associates are *Oenothera missouriensis*, *Inula ensifolia*, *Dianthus*, *Gypsophila repens*, *Armeria maritima*, *Draba dedeana*, *Saxifraga decipiens* and similar plants.

## Alpine Mouse-ear Chickweed
*Cerastium alpinum*

Caryophyllaceae

## Whitlow Grass
*Draba aizoides*

Cruciferae

Mouse-ear Chickweeds are extremely vigorous rock plants comprising xerophilous and as a rule taller species which are very effective planted out in larger spaces.

Of the lower mountain species *C. alpinum* is worthy of particular note. It is a low plant, up to 3 inches (8 cm.) high, planted only in certain sections of the rock garden set aside for true mountain alpines. A native of Scotland, the Alps, Carpathians and Pyrenees it bears comparatively large white flowers from June till August. It likes humus rich, porous soil mixed with small stones. It is easily propagated by division, root cuttings and by seed.

Drabas are low cushion rock plants from European mountains and are found at elevations of up to 11,000 feet (3,500 metres). Some species are particularly well suited for the rock garden with their low height 2 to 3 inches (5 to 8 cm.), and early flowering. They do well in poor soil in a sunny position protected against winter damp. They make nice, evergreen cushions or mats, often flowering successively from March until May. They are popular spring rock plants and good for brightening dry walls.

*D. aizoides*, a native of the Alps, is one of the earliest species and has been grown in cultivation since 1731. It forms firm, stiff rosettes of bristly leaves about 3 inches (8 cm.) high. In sheltered sunny sites it often flowers as early as the beginning of March, bearing bright yellow blossoms in compact clusters.

## *Clematis alpina*                  Ranunculaceae

*C. alpina* (syn. *Atragene alpina*) has a natural distribution extending from south and central Europe to north-east Asia. In late spring it bears a profusion of lovely blue-violet to lilac-pink flowers forming whole cascades. In our rock gardens it attains a height of about 6 feet (2 metres). The flowering period is April to May and as a rule lasts until summer.

This species requires porous to gravelly soil that is, however, humus rich with some lime and is adequately moist.

Horticulturalists have developed pink and white forms which are suitable alternatives for the type plant.

Flowering still earlier is *C. macropetala*, a native of China. It closely resembles the above species and bears bright blue-violet flowers.

*C. integrifolia* is found in south-east Europe. It has an upright growth, attaining a height of $1\frac{1}{2}$ to $2\frac{1}{2}$ feet (50 to 80 cm.), and is suitable for planting on slopes or in narrow borders where its pendant blue-violet flowers are very effective. It sends out additional shoots every year and is an exceptionally persistent plant.

Well suited for beautifying bare patches and covering large areas in the sun, as well as semi-shade are further natural species cultivated in the garden such as the white flowered *C. montana* 'Grandiflora'.

The tall *Clematis* should be associated with other creeping plants, the smaller ones can be planted in the rock garden or its vicinity.

Propagation is by seed, cuttings or grafting.

## *Cortusa matthioli*                                            Primulaceae

Ranking among the loveliest of the spring flowers, besides the rich assortment of Primulas, are many members of the Primrose family (Primulaceae). These include *Soldanella*, *Androsace*, *Dodecatheon* and also the lesser known *Cortusa*.

Cortusas are high altitude rock plants, natives of the eastern Alps and other high mountain ranges in Europe and northern Asia. They are found chiefly in damp, limy soils in semi-shaded ravines amidst taller shrubs, on the banks of streams, in screes and stony pastures, generally at elevations of 3,000 to 3,600 feet (1,000 to 1,200 metres).

These are pretty plants with lightly pubescent foliage that like damp and semi-shade. The clumps of rounded leaves bear purple-red flowers on 12 inch (30 cm.) high, upright stalks from mid-May till June. It is recommended to plant them in the rock garden in a sheltered position between stones together with taller Asiatic and other Primulas.

They prefer loose, limy, humus rich soil and a moist situation turned away from the sun or else in semi-shade.

*C. matthioli* 'Hirsuta' is a variety with delicate, soft hairs, *C. matthioli*, 'Grandiflora' bears somewhat larger flowers and *C. matthioli* 'Alba' is a rare white form.

Shortly after the seeds have ripened the plants die back and shed their leaves; therefore it is necessary to take care not to damage them when weeding or digging.

Propagation is by seed and by division of older specimens.

## *Cyclamen europaeum*                                 Primulaceae

This Cyclamen is found almost throughout the whole of southern Europe, in larger sheltered areas in the limestone Alps, in the mountain ranges on the Adriatic coast of Yugoslavia all the way to the Carpathians.

The globose or flattened tubers sometimes lie on the surface of the ground, but more often at a depth of 4 to 6 inches (10 to 15 cm.) in the wild. The plant has heart-shaped, leathery leaves, generally dark green or with lovely white patterning, and bears a profusion of single, small, lilac, pink or dark pink flowers with a lovely delicate perfume. In the garden Cyclamens should be planted in lightly shaded situations or in the rock garden, near sparsely planted bushes to resemble conditions in the wild, or in a border facing away from the sun. They require leaf mould with garden soil, limestone scree or brick rubble, some species need only garden soil on a heavy clayey base.

In winter the plants need a light protective covering of leaves. With the onset of spring they shed their leaves and care must be taken not to damage the tubers when digging the rock garden.

*C. europaeum* is a late summer flowerer, August and September. Mountain folk consider *Cyclamen* the finest of alpine plants and call them 'Alpine violets'.

All Cyclamens can be propagated by seed.

They can be associated with other smaller plants requiring semi-shade, for example hardy ferns.

# Lady's Slipper Orchid    Orchidaceae

*Cypripedium calceolus*

The lovely and popular *C. calceolus* is among the rarest plants of our semi-shaded rock gardens. A native of Europe, it is generally found in light leafy woodland or on the margins of forests where it grows in damper, limy soils rich in humus. It attains a height of about 12 to 16 inches (30 to 40 cm.) and bears one to three beautiful yellow-brown flowers in May and June.

Lady's Slipper Orchids should be planted at the edges of the rock garden or in the immediate vicinity in the partial shade of trees or amidst sparse shrubs.

The best period for transplanting is in spring so that the plant will have sufficient time to take good root. It requires beech leaf mould, in other words very humus rich soil with an admixture of lime.

Another Lady's Slipper Orchid that can be successfully grown in the garden is *C. reginae* (syn. *C. spectabile*), a native of eastern North America and slightly larger than *C. calceolus*. This species likes rather moist, humus rich soil with added peat in a slightly shaded position facing north-west. The flowers, also appearing in May and June, are a lovely pink-white.

Propagation is usually by division of rootstock. Propagation by seed is possible, but very difficult.

These orchids should be associated with plants requiring similar soil conditions, that are not too vigorous and rampant.

# Garland Flower  Thymelaeaceae

*Daphne cneorum*

Low dwarf woody plants are as indispensable in the rock garden as the other alpines. One of the great favourites is this trailing, profusely flowering shrub with dark green leaves and scented pink flowers. *D. cneorum* attains a height of 10 to 12 inches (25 to 30 cm.) and forms low shrubs resembling the Candytuft *(Iberis)*. The flowering period is in April and May, when it contributes greatly to the spring beauty of the rock garden. It is a native of central and southern Europe, where it forms extensive growths on rocks and screes in dry, sunny situations, always on a limestone base.

The trailing *Daphne* is excellent on protected slopes in the rock garden or dry wall, in partial to full sun, and stony, slightly humus rich soil with an admixture of peat. It is often associated with certain grasses *Festuca*, Blue Daisy *(Globularia cordifolia)*, Mountain Avens *(Dryas suendermannii)*, Candytuft *(Iberis sempervirens)*, Madwort *(Alyssum saxatile)* and Speedwell *(Veronica rupestris)*.

Propagation is by cuttings in July. These should be placed in a box of sand and peat and covered with glass.

Even though *Daphne cneorum* has a slow initial growth it is worthy of the notice of every rock gardener. In later years it will prove a rewarding plant with profuse and regular flowering. Older specimens, however, cannot be transplanted without risk. Sometimes, but very rarely, we also come across the white variety.

# Pink         Caryophyllaceae

*Dianthus alpinus*

Pinks are welcome additions to the garden and rockery chiefly for their lovely, abundant, pleasantly scented flowers, and also because they fill in the gap between the late spring and early summer flowering species. Of the approximately 270 species of annuals, biennials and perennials, the ones generally cultivated in the rock garden are *D. superbus* with the scent of a linden tree, and the Common Garden Pink *(D. plumarius)* with its familiar blue-green foliage, which forms large cushions and bears a profusion of flowers in May; there are a number of white, pink and red varieties. These plants will do well in any soil as long as it is not freshly fertilized, and they do not like permanent damp, as in their natural habitat they grow on rocks and sunny slopes.

One of the earliest rock garden Pinks is *D. alpinus*. It makes clumps of narrow, glossy green leaves and bears remarkably large, bright pink flowers. It requires a loamy-sandy, porous soil with good drainage and adequate moisture during the growing period. In winter, however, excessive damp is injurious. It likes a slightly sheltered position in the rock garden turned away from the direct sun. *D. alpinus* also has a creamy white variety. It should be planted in the clefts between stones, together with small species of rock plants.

Other Pinks cultivated in our rock gardens include the rarer high alpine species *D. glacialis* with narrow, stiff, green leaves and bright pink, almost sessile flowers. It requires humus rich, lime-free soil freely mixed with stones.

# Shooting Star, American Cowslip

Primulaceae

*Dodecatheon meadia*

The Shooting Stars, natives of North America, are striking rock garden plants with leaves forming rosettes like the Primrose and bearing a single stalk topped with a cluster of three to twelve or even more flowers. These resemble the blossoms of *Cyclamen europaeum* to which they are related.

A common garden species is *D. meadia* with broad, simple leaves and white-throated flowers. Nurserymen usually have two varieties of this species, namely the white *D. meadia* 'Albiflorum' and *D. meadia* 'Splendens' with somewhat larger lilac-rose flowers. *D. meadia* attains a height of 12 to 15 inches (30 to 40 cm.) and flowers in June.

Some of the other 30 or so species of *Dodecatheon* worthy of note are *D. jeffreyi* with bright purple flowers borne on 12 inches (30 cm.) long stalks and *D. pauciflorum*, only 4 to 8 inches (10 to 20 cm.) high, with pink, scented flowers.

Shooting Stars do well both in semi-shade and in the sun, in loose, porous, loamy-sandy soil, rich in humus, but also in heavier soil. The position should be sheltered from the wind. The plants are most effective alongside ornamental grasses and heath plants, chiefly because they soon die back in summer which would result in empty gaps if planted elsewhere.

Propagation is generally by seed, which is sown soon after ripening, or by division of the clumps in early autumn.

In winter the plants should be covered with a light layer of soil mixed with humus or peat. They do not tolerate lime.

# Leopards Bane  Compositae
*Doronicum columnae*

This genus comprises about 25 species of plants distinguished by yellow daisy-like flowers appearing early in spring. They are suitable for planting in herbaceous beds and as cut flowers, or else as background plants in larger rock gardens.

*D. columnae*, a native of the mountains of southern Europe and Asia Minor, is one of the loveliest of spring perennials. It is 15 to 20 inches (40 to 50 cm.) high and bears large golden-yellow flowers in April and May.

*D. caucasicum* with bright green foliage, has somewhat smaller flowers. A native of the Caucasus, it grows also in Asia Minor and its natural range extends as far as southeast Europe, where it is found in mountain forests. It attains a height of about 15 inches (40 cm.) and flowers in April to May. Though not very demanding, it does not tolerate arid conditions and burning sun; the best position is a moist situation, lightly shaded in summer by deciduous trees. This species is effective also in turf. A new form recently introduced to the market is *D. caucasicum* 'Frühlingspracht' with many golden-yellow, double flowers appearing in April and May. *D. plantagineum*, a native of western Europe, is slightly taller than the previous species and flowers somewhat later — not till May. It is a large plant growing to a height of $2\frac{1}{2}$ to 3 feet (80 to 100 cm.) and its flowers measure about $3\frac{1}{2}$ inches (8 to 9 cm.) across. It is best planted in larger gardens.

All the members of this genus require similar soil and position. Propagation is by division after flowering.

Tulips, Bleeding Heart *(Dicentra)*, *Primula*, *Iris pumila* and the Blue Alkant *(Anchusa myosotidiflora)* are good neighbours.

# Dragon's head  Labiatae
*Dracocephallum austriacum* 'Rubrum'

*D. austriacum* forms erect, sometimes drooping shrubs with stiff, much branched, densely leaved stems and large blue-violet flowers arranged in tall, loose spikes. The genus comprises about 40 species of annuals and perennials of which some are semi-shrubs. The above species is a native of central and southern Europe. It attains a height of 12 to 16 inches (30 to 40 cm.) and bears large flowers in July and August.

*D. austriacum* has a rare June flowering variety *D. austriacum* 'Rubrum' which is particularly effective in summer rock gardens.

*D. ruyschiana* is an Eurasian species with a natural distribution extending from Poland, eastern Norway and Finland south-eastwards through the Caucusus and southern Siberia all the way to Japan. It is a pretty lime-loving plant with more delicate foliage than the preceding species and the blossoms are pale to intense blue. It attains a height of 8 to 15 inches (20 to 40 cm.) and also flowers in July and August.

Both species are exceptionally persistent and are very effective in larger groups in rock gardens in the sun or beside dry walls. They prefer dry, sunny and airy positions in rich, loose, limy soil. Undemanding plants, they grow well and flower freely. In the winter months damp is very harmful.

Propagation is by division in late autumn or spring, or by seed and cuttings.

# Mountain Avens  Rosaceae

*Dryas octopetala*

*Dryas* is one of the most typical of rock garden plants, it is planted on slopes, between stones and in screes as well as in dry walls, where not only its flowers, but also its dark evergreen scalloped leaves with felted underside are very effective. The plant is a trailing sub-shrub bearing a profusion of white flowers, reminiscent of Snowdrop Anemones; if they are cut off soon after flowering the plant will bloom a second time. *Dryas* spreads quite rapidly and soon forms a thick cover over large areas in the rock garden.

The type plant is the high arctic-alpine *D. octopetala* which has several natural and garden varieties, e.g. the richly flowering *D. octopetala* var. *tenella* from Labrador with small leaves and only 2 inches (5 cm.) high. Even smaller is *D. octopetala* var. *integrifolia*, a native of the arctic mountains and one of the most valuable forms for small rock gardens; *D. octopetala* var. *vestila*, flowering from May till November, has smaller flowers but in great profusion. One of the most often found in cultivation is *D. x suendermannii* which not only has good growth but also flowers profusely.

In the wild *Dryas* usually grows on limestone formations and that is why it likes a stony, porous, slightly humus rich soil with an admixture of leaf mould or peat to retain the required moisture.

In the rock garden the plants should be placed in a position slightly turned away from the sun. They do quite well in light semi-shade.

# Heather                           Ericaceae
*Erica carnea*

The flowering of heather begins with the departing snow, the first being *E. carnea*, which bears delicate, bright pink flowers and then the Bell Heather *(E. cinerea)* with its striking red inflorescence, and ends in September and October with the flowers of the Cornish Heath *(E. vagans)*.

*E. carnea* (syn. *E. herbacea)* is a native of the eastern and central Alps, its natural distribution extending west to south-eastern France and east to the Balkans and Moravia. It is also found in the Appenines.

Spring heather makes fresh, evergreen mats and nas a lengthy flowering period from December to April. The blossoms range in colour from pink, white to red. The forms available at the grower's are e.g. *E. carnea* 'Alba' — low, 4 to 8 inches (10 to 20 cm.) compact, white; 'James Backhouse' — bright pink, very late flowering; 'King George' — — pink-red, one of the earliest to flower (often as early as late autumn); 'Rubra' — dark red, also a very early form; 'Snow Queen' — large white flowers; 'Winter Beauty' — compact, vivid pink, flowering soon after the New Year if weather conditions are suitable.

Heather does well in any light, humus rich, sandy soil that is slightly acid with an admixture of peat or heath soil, and in full sun. Bone shavings or bone meal can be added from time to time. The best position for these plants is in the heath garden.

# Fleabane, Summer Starwort

Compositae

*Erigeron aurantiacus*

The plants of this genus are closely related and show a marked resemblance to the well known Asters. They are very useful in that they flower at a time when there is a temporary lack of other blooms in the garden.

The most important of those that can be used in the rock garden is *E. aurantiacus*, a native of Turkestan, about 9 inches (20 to 25 cm.) high, making rosettes of long oval leaves and bearing orange flowers $1\frac{1}{2}$ inches (3 to 4 cm.) across. The whole plant is lightly pubescent. It needs good drainage and is particularly intolerant of winter damp, to which it often succumbs, but will grow well in ordinary garden soil. *E. aurantiacus* flowers in June and July.

This species has given rise to various pretty and profusely flowering hybrids, e.g. the yellow-red to apricot 'Asa Gray'.

Another species that can be planted in the rock garden is *E. alpinus*, only 4 to 6 inches (10 to 15 cm.) high and bearing pink-violet flowers from July to September.

Rock garden species are best in sunny, warm situations at the top of the rock garden, in the crevices of dry walls, in edgings, as well as in the free spaces of borders and garden beds where they make large thick mats. These plants look very pretty when planted with blue *Campanula* and *Veronica*.

Propagation is by division of older clumps in November or early spring or by seed.

## *Erinus alpinus*                                Scrophulariaceae

A native of the western Alps, Spain, Sardinia, the Appenines and north Africa it is naturalized on walls in some parts of this country. It is most effective in the rock garden between stones, in rock crevices and walls where it generally sows itself with ease and makes nice, profusely flowering cushions, which join to form whole mats. It is a lime lover and prefers a sunny or lightly shaded position. It attains a height of 4 inches (10 cm.). The small, lanceolate leaves form close congested mats of fresh green rosettes and the tiny flowers appearing in May and June form small, brightly coloured racemes.

The type plant *E. alpinus* has pinkish violet flowers, *E. alpinus* 'Albus' is pure white and 'Dr. Haenaele' with its bright carmine flowers is one of the loveliest forms of all.

Though not very demanding, this plant requires a sheltered situation. It likes light, sandy well drained soil and should be planted in larger groups.

Propagation is usually by seed, but as it cross-breeds easily, it fails to come true after several successive sowings. Nicely coloured individuals should be propagated by division in March or April, so that a good root system is grown before the advent of winter.

Low growing rock garden plants are good neighbours.

## Dog's Tooth Violet  Liliaceae

*Erythronium dens-canis*

Most of the species of *Erythronium* are North American but there is one Eurasian species. *E. dens-canis* is one of the bulbous plants and its flowers, appearing in March and April, are reminiscent of small exotic lilies. Its name springs from the shape of the elongate bulbs which resemble dog's teeth.

Another species in cultivation is the yellow Adder's Tongue *(E. americanum)*, a native of North America, 5 to 10 inches (12 to 25 cm.) high with dark green leaves, marbled or dotted purple-white. The solitary flowers are yellow.

*E. grandiflorum*, also a native of North America, is taller, 12 to 24 inches (30 to 60 cm.), with green, oblong leaves and large yellow or cream flowers. It is a beautiful and often cultivated species.

Dog's Tooth Violets should be planted 3 to 4 inches (7 to 10 cm.) deep, according to the size of the bulb, in loose, well drained soil rich in humus, best of all leaf mould. They are easy to grow without any special demands as to care, and soon form large groups, as they do in the wild. In larger gardens they are planted in the shade of deciduous trees, though not directly underneath them. They flower early, March to April, depending on the species and lose their foliage at the beginning of summer.

July to October is the best time for planting Dog's Tooth Violets.

Propagation is by offsets or by seed.

## Spurge, Milkwort — Euphorbiaceae

*Euphorbia myrsinites*

*Euphorbia myrsinites*, a native of the Mediterranean region, is an interesting plant forming broad clumps. Though the flowers are not particularly striking, it is a very good plant for our rock gardens, as it can be planted behind the tops of walls and in dry walls, where its whorls of blue-green leaves are most effective. In large rock gardens it frequently goes wild.

It likes dry, sunny and warm situations, good drainage and light, stony ground. In harsh winters a light protective covering is recommended. Propagation is usually by seed, which should be sown soon after ripening; it is also possible, though more difficult, to increase by division or cuttings.

Another *Euphorbia* cultivated in rock gardens is the low species from Greece, *E. capitata*, 2 to 3 inches (5 to 8 cm.) high, with prostrate, thickly leaved stalks, forming small cushions which in time spread to cover a large area.

The best known plant of this genus is *E. polychroma*, a very hardy species from south-eastern Europe. It makes hemispherical bushes with dense foliage of soft-haired, oblong leaves. The stalks bear terminal clusters of chrome-yellow leaves enveloping small yellow flowers. In sunny situations the leaves turn orange-red in the autumn.

Euphorbias are most effective as solitary plants at the edges of rock gardens, in a dry, sunny position, or amidst cushion perennials or on the tops of dry walls.

# Gentian  Gentianaceae

*Gentiana acaulis*

This genus comprises several hundred species distributed over the temperate mountain ranges of the world, at both low and high altitudes; some almost reach the border of permenant snow. Some are annual, others biennial, but the species best suited for garden cultivation are the perennials. Both alpine and arctic forms grow in various soil and climatic conditions and therefore their requirements differ widely.

The best known and most frequently cultivated are the low growing Gentians with their beautiful trumpet flowers; they make thick cushions.

The stemless Gentians of the *G. acaulis* group include the following species (considered by some authors as varieties): *G. alpina*, *G. angustifolia*, *G. clusii*, *G. kochiana* and *G. dinarica*. They are closely related and the trumpet shaped blue flowers show a marked resemblance. Distinguished by its profusion of flowers in May, frequently repeated in autumn as well, is *G. dinarica*, a native of the Alps and south-west Carpathians. The leaves are leathery, glossy, dark green, and the flowers on short stems are a somewhat lighter shade of gentian blue.

Gentians of the *acaulis* group should be planted in the rock garden in a sunny position turned slightly away from the sun, in loose soil, rich in humus, adequately moist and porous, so that it closely resembles the plants' natural environment. In cultivation freshly fertilized soil is their greatest enemy.

Propagation is by seed, division of older plants and cuttings.

# *Gentiana sino-ornata*

## Gentianaceae

The Asiatic Gentians are among the most beautiful of summer flowers in the rock garden.

They include, for instance, *G. septemfida* of Asia Minor and its hybrids, whose flowering period ends with the onset of autumn. Autumn brings with it the flowering of the loveliest Gentians known to the rock gardener.

*G. sino-ornata* was discovered by the British collector Forrest in the Yunnan mountains in south-east China. It has a prostrate growth with narrow, deep green leaves reminiscent of grass, behind which separate young plants fequently form, taking root soon after contact with the soil. In September and October the 5 to 6 inches (12 to 15 cm.) long shoots bear blue terminal flowers about 2 inches (6 cm.) long. The sepals are yellow-green on the outside with five violet tinged stripes. At this time of the year the flowers are truly striking, especially if the plants are thriving and flowering profusely.

*G. sino-ornata* requires a cooler situation in fairly heavy, lime-free, perhaps somewhat humus rich but always porous soil with a slight tendency to acidity. Suitable soil can always be prepared and a good position chosen — one where the soil will not tend to dry out even with good drainage.

Propagation of these Gentians is by division of clumps, cuttings or seed.

Good neighbours are such plants as will be of corresponding height and suitable colour.

# Crane's Bill  Geraniaceae
*Geranium argenteum*

*G. argenteum*, a native of the southern limestone Alps, is a late spring and early summer flowerer, reaching a height of 4 to 6 inches (10 to 15 cm.). It is distinguished by lobed glistening silvery leaves and violet-pink to red-violet flowers with reddish veinings. It is a beautiful alpine which should be kept dry and covered in winter. It is therefore wise to remember to give it good drainage and provide for the removal of excess water when planting.

Other Crane's Bills worthy of note are *G. sanguineum*, found wild in many parts of Europe, especially on rocky slopes. The small flowers are a rich blood red rising above congested green leaves. This is a taller species, attaining a height of 10 to 16 inches (25 to 40 cm.), and flowers in June to August. It is often planted to brighten the natural garden.

*G. cinereum*, a native of southern Europe and the Caucasus, has numerous grey-green lobed leaves and bears reddish violet flowers in July. It attains a height of 4 to 6 inches (10 to 15 cm.). It is planted in the fissures between rocks and is most effective next to white flowering plants such as *Helianthemum nummularium* 'The Bride', *Campanula carpatica* 'Alba' and similar rock plants.

Low growing Crane's Bills are planted in rock gardens and on slopes. They like humus rich, deep loose soil that does not become too dry, and a sunny situation. Taller Crane's Bills do well even in shaded positions and require little attention as they do not spread rapidly.

All are easily propagated by division in the spring or by sowing seeds.

# Avens
## Rosaceae

*Geum chiloense*

These plants are important perennials adorning early summer gardens and rockeries with their attractive bright colours.

*G. chiloense* (syn. *G. coccineum*), often grown in cultivation, is a native of the Balkans and Caucasus where it inhabits moist, subalpine meadows. It has a low, firm growth and brick red flowers appearing in June till August. It does best in sunny situations and rocky soil.

Also worthy of note is *G. sibiricum* 16 inches (40 cm.) high, with brilliant dark orange flowers appearing in May and June.

*G. montanum* is a mountain species 4 to 12 inches (10 to 30 cm.) high, making ground hugging rosettes of broad green leaves, with bright yellow flowers appearing in May and June. Though it flowers just as profusely in lowland regions as in its natural habitat, it is nevertheless a favourite rock garden plant. It is planted in the fissures between rocks in situations turned away from the sun, in humus rich, lime-free soil next to *Viola cornuta*, *G. sibiricum* and similar plants.

*G. reptans* is a beautiful and interesting high mountain species. Its large, yellow flowers are a magnificent reward for the gardener who has expended the effort to grow this difficult plant. It forms interesting lobed leaves on creeping shoots and is best grown in north-facing rock crevices in light, humus rich soil with added stone debris. In summer it likes damp, in winter it should be kept dry.

Plants can remain in one spot for three to five years, after which time they must be divided and transplanted. After flowering they should be cut back and top dressed with good porous soil.

Propagation is easy by seed or division of the clumps in early spring.

# Blue Daisy  Globulariaceae
*Globularia trichosantha*

These are low, undemanding, sub-shrubby rock plants, forming thick evergreen carpets or woody cushions. The flowers are generally blue and globose.

*G. trichosantha* is an easily grown garden plant, its natural distribution extending to Asia Minor and central Europe where it grows on sunny, grassy and stony slopes, as well as on dry meadows in the lowlands. The stalks rising from the rosettes of leaves bear heads of pale blue flowers. This species attains a height of only 4 to 12 inches (10 to 30 cm.), and flowers in May and June. It is effective planted between *Helianthemum lunulatum*, *Saponaria olivana*, *Tunica saxifraga*, *Trollius pumilus*, *Androsace* and *Festuca glauca*.

*G. cordifolia* is an interesting prostrate bushlet, woody at the base, making widespread tufts and cushions of small, dark green heart shaped leaves, bearing rounded pale blue-violet flower heads on short upright stems. It is also decorative when not in flower and is very suitable for dry rock gardens, slopes, screes and crevices where it acts as a binding agent. *G. cordifolia* has both a white and pink variety, the latter occurring only rarely in cultivation. This plant attains a height of only 2 inches (5 to 6 cm.), and flowers in May. *G. cordifolia* var. *pygmaea* is a very small form; a rare plant it measures 1½ inches (3˙ to 4 cm.) in height and bears blue flower heads in June. It does well in warm, dry and sunny positions.

*Globularia* can be planted in rock gardens on sunny slopes, in crevices and screes and do quite well even in semi-shade. The situation must be well sheltered from winter winds.

Propagation is quite easy by division or cuttings in spring, as well as by seed.

# Chalk Plant            Caryophyllaceae
*Gypsophila paniculata* 'Rosenschleier'

The best known of the Chalk Plants are the taller species that are rewarding perennials and are useful for cutting. Of the rock garden species the one that shows the greatest resemblance to the former is *G. paniculata* 'Rosenschleier' bearing masses of double pink flowers in June to August. It attains a height of about 12 to 15 inches (30 cm.), and is excellent for borders and rock gardens, as well as for dry walls, where it forms lovely thick overhangs, reminiscent of pink veils, when in flower.

*G. repens* is of alpine origin, attaining a height of 6 to 8 inches (15 to 20 cm.), and rapidly making thick carpets. It does well in stony, dry and warm situations, in limy soil. A profusion of white flowers appears in May and June and flowering often continues till early autumn.

A species that is suitable for the small rock garden and dry wall in sunny dry situations is the dwarf *G. aretioides*, a native of the Caucasus, which forms small and very hard cushions. It is truly a rarity in the rock garden and does best in fissures between stones in porous soil. The small grey-green cushions, about 1 inch (3 cm.) high, are covered with pearly white to violet tinged flowers from June till September.

Low growing Gypsophilas require porous, limy soil and a dry, sunny position.

Propagation is by seed, division and cuttings, grafting is mainly used for the tall double forms.

# Sun Rose  Cistaceae

*Helianthemum apenninum*

Helianthemums are small shrublets, usually evergreen, flowering profusely in May till July or August, the double forms till September. By cutting them back lightly as soon as the flowers are over, the flowering period can be extended till October. The colours embrace a variety of hues.

Helianthemums do well in dry and sunny situations in ordinary well drained soil, including chalk. They are natives of Europe, Asia, the Americas and north Africa, four species grow wild in Britain.

*H. apenninum* is a native of western and southern Europe and Asia Minor. It has bright yellow flowers but there are several different coloured varieties e.g. *H. apenninum* 'Carmineum' which is pink-red and the bright pink *H. apenninum* 'Roseum'. It is somewhat larger than the other species and varieties of *Helianthemum* and has very attractive silver-green foliage.

Helianthemums are popular rock plants, covered daily with masses of new flowers. In the single forms they drop their petals by evening, to be replaced by fresh blooms the following morning.

As a rule, different species and varieties of varying colours are planted together or else in the company of blue Speedwell *(Veronica)*, low Bell Flowers *(Campanula)*, Milfoil and Toadflax.

Propagation is by taking cuttings of young shoots in July or August set out in a box of sandy soil and left for the winter in a cold frame. It is also possible by seed with the exception of the double forms, but they do not come true.

# Christmas Rose  Ranunculaceae
*Helleborus niger*

Hellebores are very early flowering, fairly low perennials, comprising about twenty different species and varieties, with a natural distribution that covers central Europe, the region bordering the Mediterranean and also Asia. The first to flower is the Christmas Rose *(H. niger)*; the name comes from the black root, which bears snow-white flowers from November to March, even while the snow is still on the ground. Also attractive are the lobed evergreen leaves. In the wild it is found in the limestone Alps and occurs in two main types — the one with white, green-tinged flowers, the other with flowers that are slightly pinkish, especially at the end of flowering. In garden cultivation *H. niger* has several varieties, e.g. *H. niger* 'Grandiflorus' with large, white flowers tinted pink, and *H. niger* 'Praecox' with somewhat smaller, snow white flowers appearing 4 to 6 weeks sooner and sometimes in the late autumn at the end of November.

'Keesen' is a garden variety with a somewhat taller growth 12 to 16 inches (30 to 40 cm.), bearing large, white flowers from December to February.

Propagation is by dividing the old plants in April, seed sowing is not recommended as growth is very slow.

The flowers may need protection from the wind and rain; the best method is to cover with a cloche.

Good companions are *Anemone japonica*, *Primula*, Lungwort *(Pulmonaria)*, small ferns and other shade-loving plants.

## Lenten Rose   Ranunculaceae

*Helleborus atrorubens* (syn. *orientalis*)

*H. atrorubens* has flowers which are very variable, from purple, pink-grey to white spotted with pink, distinctive anthers. A native of Greece it flowers from February till April. It is distinguished by a good vigorous growth and rich inflorescence. There are many varieties, for example Snowdrift with white flowers and Larissa a deep rose red.

Another noteworthy garden form found also in the wild is the interesting *H. foetidus*, about 12 to 16 inches (30 to 40 cm.) high, with a rather unpleasant scent. However, the leaves are very decorative and the green and purple flowers unusual, appearing in January and February.

Hellebores grow quite slowly and do best in loose, deep, heavier, porous and rich soil, with a content of lime, which should not be too dry.

The position should be lightly shaded or at least turned away from the summer sun and kept cool. The plants should be set out in groups about 12 to 16 inches (30 to 40 cm.) apart so that the leaves cover the surrounding ground and thus prevent excess drying of the soil.

These plants do not like being disturbed but can be propagated by division of large clumps, the best time is just after flowering.

## *Hepatica triloba*                             Ranunculaceae

Hepaticas are woodland plants with no special requirements as to moisture or care. They frequently spread to form natural plant communities as in their natural habitat.

They do well in rich sandy humus rich soil with an admixture of limestone rubble. They like to remain undisturbed and if not transplanted unnecessarily they spread well and bear a profusion of flowers in February to April.

Particularly attractive are the double garden varieties *H. triloba* 'Alba' with white blossoms, 'Rosea' with pink blossoms and 'Rubra' with red blossoms and flowers in March or April.

*H. angulosa* a slightly larger plant with five-lobed leaves, bears pale blue or pinkish flowers but flowers somewhat earlier in February and March. It is especially suitable for the wild garden as it spreads freely.

The Twin Leaf *(Jeffersonia)*, *Hacquetia*, Sweet Violet *(Viola odorata)*, dwarf ferns, ornamental grasses and Anemones are often planted near them. The green leathery leaves appear after flowering and remain throughout the winter.

Propagation is by seed, sown as soon as ripe, or division of clumps in the autumn. The double forms, which can be propagated only by division after flowering, multiply fairly slowly.

# St. John's Wort  Hypericaceae

*Hypericum rhodopaeum*

St. John's Worts are rewarding rock plants and great favourites for their long flowering period and wealth of blossoms. They are good in rock gardens and dry walls, in beds amidst low-growing perennials and on slopes. All have yellow flowers with striking finely radiating stamens.

Hypericums are either herbaceous or semi-shrubs which prefer loose, light, slightly humus rich soil but grow in any good garden soil, and require warm sunny positions. Excess moisture, especially in winter, is detrimental therefore the drainage should be good. In suitable situations they live long and attain a great height.

Of those suitable for the rock garden and dry wall several low-growing species are fairly common in cultivation, e.g. *H. rhodopaeum*, which makes low, thick shrublets with blue-green foliage and bright yellow flowers borne in profusion every year as early as May.

*H. coris*, a lime lover, has narrow leaves, smaller golden yellow flowers and attains a height of only 4 to 6 inches (10 to 15 cm.). In winter it should be protected in wet weather.

*H. olympicum* is a popular and commonly cultivated *Hypericum*, 8 to 12 inches (20 to 30 cm.) high, also distinguished by a great wealth of large, orange-yellow blossoms appearing in June and July and later, sometimes until September.

St. John's Worts should be cut back after flowering and top dressed with old, well rotted compost every couple of years. In winter they require a light protective covering of fir branches or bracken.

# Evergreen Candytuft  Cruciferae
*Iberis sempervirens*

Candytufts are undemanding and profusely flowering plants that are indispensable in the rock garden and other plantings of perennials, especially on larger areas and in groups.

The species most frequently cultivated in rock gardens and borders of perennials is the Evergreen Candytuft *(I. sempervirens)* or rather several of its very pretty varieties. A native of southern Europe and Asia Minor, its branches, covered with evergreen, glossy leaves, attain a height of about 8 to 10 inches (20 to 25 cm.) and are covered with a multitude of white flowers from April till June.

*I. sempervirens* 'Snowflake' is a tall variety reaching a height of about 8 inches (20 cm.) and bearing masses of pure white flowers.

*I. sempervirens* 'Little Gem' is one of the smaller forms, about 4 inches (10 cm.) high at most, with white flowers.

Candytufts are suitable not only for rock gardens and perennial beds but also on slopes and dry walls, in the sun or light semi-shade, though here the clumps are not as thick. They like nourishing and well prepared, even stony, well drained soil. They are not particularly exacting as to moisture or warmth.

After flowering they should be cut back by about one third and will last in one spot for several years.

Annual Candytufts are propagated by seed, cuttings of *I. sempervirens* root easily and should be taken in June or September and placed in sandy soil under glass.

## *Incarvillea delavayi*                                Bignoniaceae

Natives of China and Turkestan these rank among the truly remarkable plants of our rock gardens. They are perennials with attractive foliage and unusual flowers. They do best in loamy-sandy, nutritious, warm and porous soil in positions slightly turned away from the sun but not fully shaded.

*I. delavayi*, from central China grows to a heigth of about 16 to 24 inches (40 to 60 cm.) and bears up to twelve purplish-pink flowers, $2\frac{1}{2}$ inches (5 to 7 cm.) long, on firm. stalks. These appear in May and often continue until August. The decorative leaves are reminiscent of woodland ferns. It forms seeds with ease and can be propagated by this means without any difficulty.

Damp winters are detrimental to the strong root stock and therefore the plants should have good drainage to provide adequate run-off of water and should be covered with ashes in cold areas.

Incarvilleas are excellent planted together with carpet forming perennials or ground covering woody plants, as well as in beds, borders and larger rock gardens, where they should be set out in groups of several plants spaced about 10 inches (25 cm.) apart.

All species of this genus are propagated by division of the crowns, the best time is early March or by seed sown during March in boxes or bowls. It is recommended to keep the young seedlings under glass for the winter. Balloon Flowers *(Platycodon)*, ornamental grasses, low *Coreopsis*, *Veronica rupestris*, *V. spicata*, Beard Tongue *(Pentstemon)* and Evening Primrose *(Oenothera missouriensis)* make good neighbours.

# Dutch Iris                                          Iridaceae

*Iris* × *hollandica*

This is a lovely Iris with globose tuber resembling a bulb, it belongs to the same group as the well known English and Spanish Irises.

There are many forms in various colours ranging from creamy white, yellow, bronze to blue and violet. 'Bulbous' Irises are planted in the autumn, September and October, in rich porous soil in a sunny position. They should be put at a depth of 4 inches (10 cm.) spaced 6 inches (15 cm.) apart, in groups, preferably with small rock plants or ornamental grasses where their large and beautiful flowers will be most effective.

The Dutch Iris should be dug up each year, when the leaves have faded, and replanted in fresh soil during October but the English Iris can be left until the bed is very crowded, when they should be lifted and replanted; the best time is in August to September.

They are most effective planted amidst ornamental grasses and cushion perennials. Though hardy, it is recommended to cover the soil with dry peat in winter.

Propagation of all Irises is by offsets or by division of the rhizomes and they thrive wherever Hyacinths or Tulips can be successfully cultivated.

# Lavender                                           Labiatae
*Lavandula officinalis*

Lavender is a well known and popular evergreen shrublet with grey-green aromatic leaves and blue flowers, as a rule. The genus, which comprises 25 species, is a native of the Mediterranean area, its natural distribution extending to the Canary Islands as well as to India. The two species mainly coming into consideration for garden cultivation as ornamentals are *L. latifolia* and *L. officinalis* (syn. *spica*).

*L. officinalis* is eminently suitable for hedges, edgings, borders and the rock garden. It reaches a height of 10 to 20 inches (25 to 50 cm.) and bears lilac-blue blossoms arranged in a loose spikelet. The flowering period is in June and July. A more striking inflorescence marks the silver-blue form 'Dwarf Blue' — 16 inches (40 cm.) high at the most, the dark lilac-blue 'Hidcote Blue' — only 12 to 16 inches (30 to 40 cm.) high, the dark blue 'Munstead' — 16 inches (40 cm.) high, the delicate pink 'Rosea' — 16 inches (40 cm.), and the pure white 'Alba' — 16 inches (40 cm.).

These plants are excellent on dry walls in the sun and on slopes where they help retain the soil. They require a dry, loamy-sandy, limy soil that has good porosity, for excess moisture is detrimental. They are hardy plants, but if they should, nevertheless be frost-bitten in particularly severe winters they can be cut back strongly in spring. This spontaneously regenerates them and they spread out anew.

Propagation can be by seed, but the individual forms are better propagated by cuttings.

# Edelweiss  Compositae

*Leontopodium alpinum*

The Edelweiss, symbol of high alpine flora, is one of the most popular rock plants in our rock gardens. The genus comprises about 40 species; one of the best known is the Alpine Edelweiss. The genus is also found in the Pyrenees, Carpathians, the Balkans, Turkestan, Afghanistan, the Himalayas and even in Japan. It shows great variety in the wild and there are great differences in the flowers. They are always characterized, however, by compact growth which is not always true of the Edelweiss cultivated in our gardens and rockeries, where the soil is generally much richer than in their natural habitat. In nutritious soils they lose their silvery-white colouration, do not develop the woolly hairs and are marked by vigorous growth, thus losing their distinctive, high alpine character. The choice of a suitable position is therefore of great importance if the plant is to develop into the typical alpine type with white-felted leaves arranged in a ground hugging rosette. The best place in the rock garden is between limestone rocks or in screes of light, poor, limy soil that is porous, slightly humus rich and mixed with gravel; in full sun it flowers profusely from June till August.

Propagation is by seed, best sown in February, when it is sure to germinate, and also by careful division of older clumps in autumn.

It is usually associated with certain Saxifrages, *Campanula pusilla*, *Thymus serpyllum* 'Splendens', summer species of Gentians and similar alpines.

# Bitter-root  Portulacaceae

*Lewisia cotyledon*

These plants, whose natural distribution embraces the dry plains and semi-deserts of North America, will thrive in cultivation only if their special needs are fulfilled as far as possible. The genus comprises about 20 different species. In their natural habitat they have a period of absolute drought in the summer and it is therefore necessary to try to provide the same conditions in cultivation.

*L. cotyledon*, a native of California, has a branched inflorescence. The flowers, borne on long stems up to 10 inches (25 cm.) high, are pink and white purplish veins and appear in June till August. The leaves form rosettes 6 to 10 inches (15 to 25 cm.) across. Like all the plants of this genus *L. cotyledon* is one of the gems of the rock garden.

In the rockery Lewisias require a thoroughly porous, very stony, sandy-humus rich soil free of lime, and a warm, light situation but not in direct sun, the best position of all is slightly turned away from the sun, e.g. in a rock crevice or stony rubble, but always in soil with very good drainage. They also do well in dry walls if protected from summer and winter damp; it is definitely recommended to cover them with transparent foil or glass in winter.

Propagation is by seed, either sown as soon as ripe in the late summer or not till February if under glass.

Lewisias are either set out individually or in the company of small alpines.

## Toadflax  Scrophulariaceae
*Linaria alpina*

## Slipper Flower
*Calceolaria biflora*

Toadflaxes are small leaved, usually creeping plants with no particular demands. They spread quickly and are good for strengthening dry walls and slopes and to decorate the rock garden. One of the best known and most commonly cultivated Toadflaxes is *L. alpina*, a native of the Italian Alps, distinguished by a long flowering period from early summer till autumn. The blossoms are fairly large and coloured blue-violet. It attains a height of about 4 inches (10 cm.) and makes large thick clumps. This species is especially suited for dry walls, in the sun and semi-shade, together with *Sedum*, *Sempervivum* and *Campanula*. It is easily propagated by division.

*Calceolaria biflora*, a native of South America, is a rock plant with leaves arranged in the form of a rosette and yelow, sometimes red-speckled flowers borne on 4 to 6 inches (10 to 15 cm.) high stalks — frequently two to a stalk. The flowering period is from June till July. *C. biflora* crossed with *C. polyrrhiza* produced the lovely large-flowered hybrid 'John Innes', bearing yellow blossoms with chocolate brown spots.

In rock gardens Calceolarias do best in light semi-shade or in positions sheltered from the midday sun, and require light, loose, humus rich and slightly acid soil, not too dry and with good drainage. It is easily propagated by seed, or by division of root stock in spring.

# Flax  Linaceae

*Linum salsoloides*

Flaxes are worth planting in the rock garden for their ease of cultivation and continual flowering from May till July, often till September. As a rule they are finely leaved herbs making clumps of stiff stems, sometimes woody at the base, and bearing large flowers in loose clusters.

*L. salsoloides*, a native of the Italian Alps and other mountains in the Mediterranean area, attains a height of about 8 inches (20 cm.) and makes prostrate, pendant clumps, covered from May till June with lovely white pale mauve centred flowers. It is a rock plant of neat and non-invasive habit, suitable for the rock garden and dry walls in the sun.

The most fequently cultivated of the other Flaxes is *L. perenne;* its natural distribution extends from southern Europe to central and northern USSR and North America. A comparatively tall perennial, about 12 to 20 inches (30 to 50 cm.) high, the groups of stems are covered with fine, grey-green foliage. The bright blue blossoms, up to 1 inch (3 cm.) across, appear in June and July; the flowering, however, is often repeated.

All Flaxes are of light, airy construction and are most effective planted as solitaries or in groups together with low perennials, both in large rock gardens and dry walls. They require a warm position, even on a slope, and good garden soil, best of all with lime. They are quite tolerant of continually dry conditions.

Propagation is easy by seed, *L. salsoloides* can also be propagated by cuttings.

# Evening Primrose             Oenotheraceae

*Oenothera missouriensis*

*O. missouriensis*, a native of the southern part of North America, is a prostrate plant with thick, dark red stems bearing narrow leaves from whose axils rise enormous, sulphur-yellow flowers, appearing from early summer till late autumn. As its name indicates, the Evening Primrose is a night-flowerer, new blossoms open with the advent of the evening, to make the rock garden appear as if lights had been turned on. The glow lasts till morning when it dies as the sun takes over.

Attaining a height of 6 to 8 inches (15 to 20 cm.), these plants are excellent in rock gardens, dry walls or low cushion plantings. They are indispensable companions of *Campanula carpatica*, *Veronica spicata*, *Nepeta mussini* and *Gentiana cruciata*.

They should be set out in the sun in dry and poor soils containing lime. In too rich soils they become rampant. The plants die back in winter.

A similar, but earlier flowering species is *O. trilobata*, forming a large clump of finely cut leaves resembling those of the dandelion, and bearing huge, pale yellow flowers over a long period. It is a self-sowing plant and thus often changes its position in the rock garden.

Evening Primroses are propagated by seed, cuttings and division of older clumps.

# Golden Drop  Boraginaceae
*Onosma albo-roseum*

Of the about 70 species of the genus *Onosma*, natives of southern Europe, north Africa, and eastern Asia, only a few of the most interesting are cultivated in the rockery.

*O. albo-roseum*, a native of Asia Minor, has large tubular white flowers with red or blue markings appearing in May or June. The leaves make rosettes 6 to 8 inches (15 to 20 cm.) high.

*O. cassium*, a native of northern Syria, is a larger species attaining a height of 12 to 16 inches (30 to 40 cm.). The flowers, borne in May and June, are pale yellow.

*O. stellulatum* (syn. *helveticum*), a native of southern Europe and Asia Minor, grows to a height of 6 to 8 inches (15 to 20 cm.) and has tall erect stems and yellow flowers in May and June.

*O. tauricum* (syn. *stellulatum* var. *tauricum*) of south-east Europe shows a marked resemblance to the preceding species. It has narrow, pubescent leaves, lemon to golden yellow flowers and is about 12 inches (30 cm.) high.

These plants do best in the sun on dry walls, in sloping rock gardens and in rock crevices. All like a well-drained soil, limestone rubble or limestone rocks and a position that is warm and sheltered, especially against constant moisture chiefly in winter, but also in damp summers.

Propagation may be by seed, but also by division and taking cuttings from nonflowering shoots. Transplanting is not well tolerated by older plants.

Good companions are Flaxes *(Linum)*, Bell Flowers *(Campanula)*, Speedwell *(Veronica)*, Globularia and other unexacting, xerophilic plants.

# Paeony  Ranunculaceae

*Paeonia tenuifolia*

The most familiar Paeonies are classed into several groups. The first comprises those that are hybrids of *P. officinalis*. It is a native of southern and central Europe and blooms in May bearing large ruby-red flowers. There are several garden varieties and the height is never more than 16 inches (40 cm.).

The second group embraces the so-called Chinese Paeonies. *P. lactiflora*, natives of east Siberia and China's western mountains. The various forms are single, semi-double as well as double and have a wide range of colours.

The third group comprises the so-called tree Paeonies, *P. suffruticosa* is considered to be the loveliest of all the Paeonies. Mature plants reach a height of about 4 to 5 feet (1.50 metres) and like a sheltered position in the sun. They bear single and double flowers in many different colours including yellow.

*P. tenuifolia*, a native of southern Europe, Asia Minor and the Caucasus, belongs to a further group, the so-called botanical Paeonies. It grows to a height of 12 to 18 inches (30 to 45 cm.) and has characteristic crowded, finely divided leaves and bright crimson flowers with 8 to 10 petals. There is also a pink variety — *P. tenuifolia* 'Rosea'. A hardy species, it thrives in any loamy-sandy soil in a warm, sunny situation. It can be planted both in beds and larger rock gardens.

In general, Paeonies prefer a soil well fertilized with natural manure or well-rotted compost. The best time for transplanting is from mid-September till the end of October. During dry spells they require frequent watering.

# Alpine Poppy  Papaveraceae

*Papaver alpinum kerneri*

The large family of Poppies embraces a vast number of ornamental and attractive plants — annuals and perennials, single and double, suitable for borders and beds as well as rock gardens.

Excellent plants for the garden and rockery are the Icelandic and Alpine Poppies. They are very long-lived and hardy, for in their natural habitat, in the mountains, they frequently grow under the most difficult conditions.

The Alpine Poppy *(P. alpinum)*, a native of the Pyrenees, Alps and Carpathians, only 6 to 8 inches (15 to 20 cm.) high and flowering from May till August. One of the loveliest of rock garden Poppies is also attractive for its dainty silver-grey foliage. It bears flowers in many colours, pale yellow, orange, pink and white.

The Iceland Poppy *(P. nudicaule)*, a native of Iceland, blooms from May till August, the flowers are shades of yellows and oranges. Propagation is by seeds, sown in spring or autumn, the later being the best time.

These remarkably vigorous Poppies with their fairly strong rootstock serve to strengthen the scree in rock gardens and should be planted with annual plants such as the Alpine Toadflaxes *(Linaria alpina)*.

All Poppies like a slightly moist well drained, not too freshly fertilized soil with a content of lime, and either a sunny or lightly semi-shaded position.

# Phlox  Polemoniaceae

*Phlox divaricata*

Phloxes are mostly natives of America where they grow abundantly on river banks. They are divided into low Phloxes, carpeting Phloxes, medium Phloxes and tall Phloxes, and their uses in the garden and rockery are manifold.

*P. divaricata*, a native of thin woods from Quebec to Florida, is a medium-tall plant, 8 to 12 inches (20 to 30 cm.) high, with an erect growth. The lilac-blue flowers appear in May and June. It is suitable for larger rock gardens, borders and beds. It needs a deep, neutral to slightly acid, loose, humus rich soil. *P. divaricata* has several varieties and forms e.g. *P. divaricata* var. *laphamii* with somewhat larger, dark violet flowers, the white *P. divaricata* 'Alba' and the blue-violet 'Violet Queen' which is slighly smaller, only 4 to 6 inches (10 to 15 cm.) in height. These Phloxes do not like an exceedingly hot and dry situation in summer. If conditions are favourable they soon spread over large areas. Another medium-tall Phlox is the garden hybrid *P. arendsii*, attaining a height of at least 16 inches (40 cm.) and has erect stems. The flowering period is from June till August, thus filling the gap between the end of the spring flowering and beginning of the summer flowering Phloxes. It has several forms, e.g. the carmine-pink 'Hanna', the bright lavender-blue, pink-eyed 'Hilda', the lilac-pink 'Inge' and others.

Propagation of Phloxes is by division and cuttings. If left in one place for several years they bear smaller flowers.

# Moss Pink                          Polemonicaceae

*Phlox subulata*

An outstanding representative of the carpeting Phloxes is *P. subulata* 'Temiskaming'. This product of Swedish cultivation is a striking bright carmine, attracting the notice of every rock garden lover. An evergreen form, it is about 3 inches (10 cm.) high and makes carpets covered with a flood of brightly coloured blossoms.

The carpeting Phloxes are natives of eastern North America. The natural distribution, however, extends all the way to Lake Michigan. There they grow in thin woods in drier soils, where they make huge cushiony growths.

Of the many garden varieties of *P. subulata* (syn. *setacea*) worthy of note are the following: 'Atropurpurea' — dark carmine-pink to carmine-red with a dark eye, 'Daisy Hill' — salmon-pink with red eye, 'G. F. Wilson' — pale slate-blue, somewhat less crowded, taller and with softer, longer leaves, 'Samson' — making compact cushions completely covered with salmon-pink flowers, and the lovely white 'Maischnee'.

Phloxes are most effective in a combination of the various forms with their varying colours. They do well in any sandy and stony soil in the sun with adequate warmth and moisture.

Propagation is by division, cuttings and small tufts of foliage, which are put in sandy soil to root in spring and summer.

# Horned Rampion             Campanulaceae

*Phyteuma scheuchzeri*

This interesting mountain perennial is one of 29 species growing in central and southern Europe on limestone formations and in acid ground, at altitudes from 600 to 6,750 feet (200 to 2,250 metres).

*P. scheuchzeri* attains a height of 6 to 16 inches (15 to 40 cm.) and forms a rosette of ovate, basal leaves. The stem leaves are narrowly lanceolate and sparse. The dark blue flowers at the top of the stem are arranged in a congested sphere, creating the impression of a single blossom measuring up to 1 inch (3 cm.) across and containing 20 or more individual flowers. The flowering season is in June and July, enlivening the summer beauty of the rock garden. This plant is suitable only for the natural rock garden in the company of *Androsace*, *Campanula carpatica*, *Campanula pustilla* 'Alba', Cinquefoil *(Potentilla)*, Crane's Bill *(Geranium subcaulescens)*, and also the blue-grey *Festuca* grasses, amidst which it grows in its natural habitat in the alpine meadows.

*Phyteuma* can be planted in light as well as partially shaded positions. The soil should be a light loam with good drainage and with a content of lime. Otherwise there are no special requirements.

It makes self-sown seedlings with ease and appears unexpectedly in various new spots. It can be propagated by division but the best method is by seed. It is recommended to mix the very fine seeds with sand before sowing to prevent excessive crowding.

## Balloon Flower      Campanulaceae

*Platycodon grandiflorum*

Though not a real rock plant, the Balloon Flower is often cultivated in larger rock gardens despite its great size, 12 to 18 inches (30 to 60 cm.). The swollen, angular buds open up into large, broad, five-pointed, bell-shaped flowers coloured pale blue, or white in *P. grandiflorum* 'Album'.

This very variable species has several garden varieties e.g. *P. grandiflorum* 'Nanum', only 3 to 4 inches (8 to 10 cm.) high and excellent for the rock garden, 'Mariesii' measuring 8 to 12 inches (20 to 30 cm.) with large, intense blue flowers, and 'Perlmutterschale', 20 inches (50 cm.) high with magnificient blue-pink blossoms.

All Platycodons flower from July till August and are very effective in mixed groups of perennials in borders, at the foot of dry walls and in large rock gardens which are enlivened by their wealth of striking and attractive flowers. The roots are pulpy and tuberous. They do well in sunny positions, drier in winter, and also in partial shade — however, not directly under trees. They like a loamy-sandy and not too poor soil that is kept dry during the growing period, in other words, almost any good garden soil.

*P. grandiflorum* is generally propagated by seed, which are planted out in October or early spring; it is rarely divided because it does not like being disturbed.

## *Primula auricula*  Primulaceae

The large genus of Primulas embraces a wide assortment of plants, many of which are among the most rewarding and attractive spring flowerers in the garden and rockery. For easier orientation the individual species are grouped into twenty sections. Belonging to one of these is the well known *P. auricula* whose new garden varieties with their wide range of bright colours are becoming very popular again.

The section Auricula also embraces several popular species grown only in the rock garden where they make cushions of little, thick, usually dentate leaves, e.g. *P. minima*, the smallest of the European Primulas, very dainty with rose-violet flowers, and the type plant *P. auricula*. The latter grows chiefly on limestone formations in the Alps, Apennines and west Carpathians, its natural distribution extending up to elevations of 6,300 feet (2,100 metres), where it makes groups of rosettes in rock crevices. In cultivation it requires a heavier, humus rich soil mixed with small stones and limestone rubble. In April and May it bears lovely, fragrant, yellow flowers.

Auriculas will not grow in garden soil that is too rich. They like an eastern to south-eastern position in cracks between stones in dry walls, as well as on level ground at the foot of the rock garden or on a slight slope, however, not in full sun.

*P. auricula* is propagated by seed and division of older clumps in July. True Auriculas should be planted together with more precious alpine rock plants.

# Bardfield Oxlip │ Primulaceae

*Primula elatior*

*P. elatior* grows in the wild in almost all of Europe including eastern England. It requires partial shade, north-facing situation and a loose, moist soil. The flowers of the natural species are sulphur-yellow, slightly pendant and without fragrance. Garden varieties have large up to 1½ inches (4 cm.) across, fragrant flowers with a yellow central eye. Their position should be lightly shaded.

The years have produced several garden varieties marketed under various names such as *P. elatior* 'Grandiflora' — 6 to 8 inches (15 to 20 cm.) high with profuse flowers, *P. elatior* 'Pacific Giant' or 'Colosea' 6 to 10 inches (15 to 25 cm.) high with large blossoms in a wide range of colours, *P. elatior* 'Vierländer' 6 to 8 inches (15 to 20 cm.) high with large golden-yellow flowers, and other cultivated forms with flowers up 2 inches (6 cm.) across in brilliant hues.

Resembling the above Primulas but with sessile flowers are the Common Primrose *(P. vulgaris)*, the type plant bearing a wealth of sulphur-yellow flowers in early spring, before any of the others. The garden hybrids have large flowers in various colours. There are also the more precious double varities; these, however, spread much more slowly and sometimes are even prone to disease or are not completely hardy.

Common Primroses also like a lightly shaded, warmer and not too dry place and a damp, well drained soil with humus.

Propagation is by seed or division.

## *Primula rosea*                                     Primulaceae

This species is a native of the north-west Himalayas, Kashmir and Afghanistan, where it grows at altitudes of 8,000 to 12,000 feet (2,700 to 4,000 metres) on the banks of streams, large meadows and often on the very edge of melting snow fields.

This magnificent early spring flowerer glows in the garden like a gem, with its salmon-pink blossoms.

The flowering period is from March till April and in cultivation, as in the wild, it does well in damp situations in heavier, clayey soil rich in humus. The leaves appear after flowering.

Generally grown in gardens are *P. rosea* 'Grandiflora' — somewhat taller with larger flowers, the cultivated form 'Gigas' with unusually large, carmine flowers, the slightly darker 'Micia Visser de Geer' and several other cultivated forms. All attain a height of 6 to 8 inches (15 to 20 cm.).

*P. rosea* does best near water or in damp soil, then it can stand full sun and where the conditions are suitable it will remain in one place for several years. Sometimes it makes self-sown seedlings and spreads to form very thick clumps bearing a profusion of flowers. It is most effective in larger groups near a pool; the Marsh Marigold *(Caltha palustris)* and neat low grasses are good companions.

Propagation is by seed sown as soon as ripe when germination is best, or by dividing the larger clumps.

# Pasque Flower                                Ranunculaceae

*Pulsatilla vulgaris amoena*

Whoever has seen this plant in full flower in its natural habitat will never forget it. The flowering period, which is very early, is influenced in the wild not only by the climatic conditions but also, and chiefly by the altitude of the site. The purple flowers generally appear in March, the plants growing in warmer, sheltered positions being the first to flower.

Cultivation is easy, if the special requirements as to soil and position are fulfilled. Failure can be expected only if the plants are put in immature soil with too much humus or if they are given too much water during the summer rest period. Pasque Flowers require some humus in the soil, but only the natural kind produced in time by the surrounding plants, in other words a fairly poor humus, and chalky soil.

They do best on sunny, open slopes or at the top of the rockery in loose, porous soil with faultless drainage.

These plants are welcome inhabitants of the rock garden not only for their flowers which are a riot of colour, but also for their decorative leaves throughout most of the growing period and after flowering also for their shaggy seeds. There is frequently a second flowering in the autumn, the blossoms being equally attractive, though smaller than those in spring.

Propagation is by seed as soon as ripe.

## *Pulsatilla vulgaris* 'Slavica'          Ranunculaceae

*P. vulgaris* 'Slavica', a native of the Carpathians is one of the loveliest and most commonly cultivated of the Pulsatillas.

The leaves are larger than in the other species and less divided, the flowers are large, pale violet, erect, and slightly pendant when fully opened. This plant grows in rocks rich in humus as well as in rock crevices where other plants have a hard time struggling to survive.

Mention should be made of at least some of the species, many varieties, forms and cultivars: *P. vulgaris* 'Amoena' with dark, many-partite leaves and bearing large, red-violet flowers somewhat later than *P. vulgaris* 'Slavica', the attractive pure white *P. vulgaris* 'Alba', the velvety red *P. vulgaris* 'Rubra', and the pure pink *P. vulgaris* 'Mrs. van der Elst'.

All Pulsatillas do best in sunny, open places in the rock garden in deep, not too dry and not too wet, stony soil with humus, amidst ornamental grasses, carpeting Thyme *(Thymus)* and cushion Stonecrop *(Sedum)*.

When planting *P. vulgaris* 'Slavica', which grows on limestone formations in the wild, limestone or builder's rubble should be added to the soil; the other forms do not require the addition of lime.

## Pyrenean Primrose         Gesneriaceae

*Ramonda pyrenaica*

*R. pyrenaica* (syn. *myconi*) is a remarkable and rare species which survived as an endemic in the Pyrenees from before the Ice Ages when many other species of the tropical family Gesneriaceae were widespread in Europe.

*R. pyrenaica* forms a low rosette, about 8 inches (20 cm.) across, of large evergreen, ovate leaves, with deeply toothed margins and rough surfaces. The top surface is dark green, the undersurface covered with copper-coloured hairs. The flowers, one to five, on 4 inch (10 cm.) stems are lavender-blue with bright yellow anthers. Appearing from late May till July, depending on the locality, they resemble the well known African Violet *(Saintpaulia)* and have a faint scent.

*R. pyrenaica* also has rare white or pink varieties but the blue is the prettiest.

Ramondas do best in vertical north or east facing banks between stones, or in the crevices of damp rock walls, in other words in positions turned away from the sun, but not shaded. Good companions are small ferns and related species such as *Haberlea rhodopea* or *Moehringia muscosa*.

They should be planted in humus rich, clayey soil mixed with brick rubble or small stones.

Propagation is usually by seed or leaf cuttings in early spring.

## Alpine Buttercup　　　　　　　　Ranunculaceae
*Ranunculus montanus*

## *Townsendia formosa*　　　　　　Compositae

An interesting genus of alpines are the small Buttercups. Chief of these is the Alpine Buttercup. *R. montanus*, which grows to a height of 4 to 6 inches (10 to 15 cm.) and in May and June bears glossy, rich yellow flowers, a lovely supplement to the azure blue of the spring Gentians. It also has a nice double form. The soil should be damp, with lime and stones. Propagation is by seed.

*Townsendia* comes from the Rocky Mountains of North America; in spring they bear violet Aster-like blossoms, and often have a repeated flowering.

Of the Townsendias the one most reminiscent of tiny Asters is *T. formosa* with lovely pale-violet flowers on short stems; it blooms from May till early summer.

Townsendias are mainly grown in miniature rock gardens or in special parts of larger rock gardens. They are planted in small spaces among stones which protect the roots and neck from freezing and from winter damp.

All species like a very sunny, warm position and not too poor, sandy soil with faultless drainage.

Propagation is generally by seed but also by cuttings.

Good neighbours are smaller rock plants.

# Rose                                                     Rosaceae

*Rosa multiflora* 'Sweet Pink'

The Roses also embrace a number of miniature, so-called dwarf roses which, though bearing smaller blossoms, flower profusely throughout the whole summer. They make branched shrubs 8 to 12 inches (20 to 30 cm.) high, sometimes more, covered with small, fine leaflets and are excellent in rock gardens as well as in flowerpots and boxes on the window-sill or balcony.

'Sweet Pink' is a somewhat taller form bearing a wealth of double pink flowers every year till late in the autumn.

One of the oldest species is the well known rose-red *R. chinensis* (syn. *rouletti*), semi-double, 4 to 6 inches (10 to 15 cm.) high, covered with tiny blossoms from May till November.

The garden variety 'Baby Maskerade' is a recent miniature changing its colour from a copper-yellow bud through red, srraw-yellow to fiery-red or peach-red.

'Zwergkönig' is also a recent form with decorative foliage and elegant buds, which slowly open into remarkably persistent red blooms, the colour remaining the same from beginning to end.

These dwarf Roses have the same requirements as bush roses and are effective planted amidst dwarf shrubs, conifers and not too striking rock plants.

Propagation is by cutting or budding.

# Soapwort  Caryophyllaceae

*Saponaria ocymoides*

Only 2 to 4 inches (5 to 10 cm.) high, *S. ocymoides* has fairly large, pinkish-red flowers on short scapes. It makes firm, dark green cushions of fleshy, coniferous leaflets covered from June to August with a profusion of flowers.

*S. ocymoides* likes full sun and loose, porous, loamy-sandy soil. It is eminently suitable for rock gardens, walls and spaces between stones and very effective in the company of *Campanula*, *Gypsophila*, *Arenaria* and like plants.

After flowering it is recommended to top dress the mats with sandy soil.

Propagation is by cuttings or by seed.

*S. caespitosa* is another pretty Soapwort which makes low cushions — only 2 to 4 inches (5 to 8 cm.) high — the small linear leaves forming a rosette from which pink flowers rise in June and July.

*S. pumila*, also known as *Silene pumilio*, forms low, about 1 inch (3 cm.) high dense cushions, covered in June and July with sessile pink flowers. This pretty and rare rock plant, which does best in light semi-shade, in acid, humus rich, non-drying soil free of lime, is suitable for the rock garden and spaces between stones in the company of similar, delicate plants.

Propagation is by division, seed and cuttings.

# Rockfoil, Silver Saxifrage

Saxifragaceae

*Saxifraga aizoon*

The Rockfoils are well known and popular plants in our rock gardens. This large genus is divided into several sections with more or less the same characteristics and requirements which must be taken into account when planting them in our gardens and rockeries.

The first section, Dactyloides, comprises the Mossy Saxifrages making dense green cushions of smaller or larger evergreen rosettes.

The second section Euaizoonia, consists of the Silver Saxifrages; they have rosettes of firm, leathery leaves with lime-encrusted margins. The flowers, in large branching panicles are white. The members of this section are to be found on limestone rocks in many parts of Europe and North America where they generally grow in positions turned away from the sun, often in the company of semi-shadeloving plants.

The type plant *S. aizoon* is widespread throughout the Alps, and has rosettes of firm, grey-green to silvery leaves, from which rise stems topped with sprays of white flowers in late spring. This species has several cultivated garden varieties, e.g. *S. aizoon* 'Rosea' with slightly smaller pale pink flowers, the carmine *S. aizoon* 'Splendens' and the pale, sulphur-yellow *S. aizoon* 'Lutea'.

Propagation is by division and by seed.

## *Saxifraga marginata*  Saxifragaceae
## *Saxifraga x paulinae*

The Kabschias and Englerias are considered the rarest of the Saxifrages by cultivators. The two sections have much in common and are often listed jointly in horticultural catalogues. They comprise a large number of species and are rightfully ranked among the loveliest and daintiest of Saxifrages.

*S. marginata*, a native of the Appennines, eastern Alps and Balkans, has somewhat broader, grey-green foliage and sprays of large white flowers.

Other Kabschias are the easy-growing, very early, yellow *S. paulinae*, *S. apiculata*, *S. elisabethae*, *S. haagii*, *S. sancta*, *S. dalmatica* and many more.

They are very suitable for rock gardens in north or north-east-facing positions, best of all in rock crevices or scree filled with a mixture of stone rubble, well-rotted leaf mould, fine sieved soil and a little sand. For the more exacting plants which require more moisture it is recommended to add finely chopped sphagnum moss and brick rubble; fine gravel should be placed around the neck of the plant. The flowering period begins as early as January and continues through February.

Kabschia and Engleria Saxifrages are propagated by seeds, division of larger plants or cuttings, the best times being spring or early autumn.

They should be planted together with delicate rock plants or in the company of several different species and varieties of Kabschias, best of all in groups.

# London Pride  Saxifragaceae

*Saxifraga umbrosa*

One of the easiest plants to grow is London Pride *(S. umbrosa)*, a native of Ireland and the Pyrenees. It makes large rosettes of leathery green leaves, mat as well as glossy. In June till August the much branched stalks are covered with a cloud of tiny pale pink blossoms. It will grow in almost any part of the garden and will tolerate semi-shade.

One of the loveliest Rockfoils of this section is the well known garden minature *S. umbrosa* 'Elliott's Variety'. Its multi-branched stems, rising to a height of about 4 to 5 inches (10 to 12 cm.) bear a mass of dark pink flowers in June till August. It is an indispensable and popular plant for the semi-shaded parts of the garden and rockery.

Other garden varieties are *S. umbrosa* 'Serratifolia' with longer, broadly dentate leaves, and *S. umbrosa* 'Variegata' with pink-white spotted leaves.

Like all other Saxifrages these are evergreen and make good ground cover both in sunny and slightly shaded positions. They are often used as a substitute for turf and are excellent as border plants in the shaded parts of the garden. Smaller species and varieties are planted in some of the larger spaces between rocks in the rock garden, in positions facing away from the sun, in partial shade.

They are propagated by division, the individual rosettes soon grow into larger clumps.

# Squill  Liliaceae
*Scilla sibirica*

*S. sibirica* is not a native of Siberia as its name would indicate, but of the Balkans, Asia Minor, and southern and central USSR. It is a very popular bulbous plant, suitable for the rock garden, as underplanting for ornamental shrubs or in the woodland part of the garden. Besides the type plant, which bears brilliant blue flowers in March and April, there are also several other popular varieties e.g. the white *S. sibirica* 'Alba' and *S. sibirica* 'Taurica', an earlier and taller form with attractive pale blue flowers.

A truly distinctive member of the genus is *S. tubergeniana*, a native of north-west Persia. It is more robust than *S. sibirica* and is the earliest to flower; it has a profusion of pale blue flowers with darker bands.

Very different from the foregoing species and often planted among hardy ferns is the Spanish Bluebell, *S. campanulata* (syn. *hispanica*), a native of the Iberian Peninsula. It bears clusters of bell-shaped flowers from May till June. The type plant is blue-violet, but the numerous garden forms may be various shades of blue and pink or white.

Squills, like all other bulbous plants, are planted in the autumn into loose, porous garden soil with humus.

Propagation is by offsets and by seed sown in compost; they may take up to four years to flower.

# Stonecrop  Crassulaceae

*Sedum spurium* 'Superbum'

Stonecrops are well known and undeservedly neglected rock plants, whose flowers brighten the sparser summer and autumn floral display of the garden and rockery. They are usually low-growing plants.

*S. spurium* has a wide natural distribution in Europe. It is indispensable in its cultivated varieties for planting in the spaces between stones, especially in large rock gardens, borders, on banks and in walls. It thrives both in the sun and in semi-shade, forming large, compact, ground-hugging mats of dark green or copper leaves and bearing a wealth of flowers. These are white in *S. spurium* 'Album', purplish-red in *S. spurium coccineum*, and bright pink in *S. spurium* 'Roseum Superbum'.

Stonecrops embrace many species and varieties, attractive both for their flowers of various hues and for their leaves which are also attractively coloured. They are unpretentious plants which will grow even where other plants will not, because of arid conditions, strong sunlight or too poor soil.

Propagation is by division, cuttings and by seed.

Good neighbours in the rock garden are *Aster dumosus*, Bell Flowers *(Campanula)*, *Festuca* grasses, Catmint *(Nepeta)*, Houseleek *(Sempervivum)*, Whitlow Grass *(Draba)*, smaller Chalk Plants *(Gypsophila)*, *Hutchinsia*, and silver Saxifrages.

# Houseleek　　　　　　　　　　　　　　Crassulaceae

*Sempervivum arachnoideum*

*Sempervivum ornatum*

The botanical name *Sempervivum* means 'always alive' and the Houseleeks are very hardy and tenacious plants.

Their beauty rests chiefly in their great diversity of shape and colouration. Species which have some red leaves generally bear pink flowers, green-leaved ones usually have yellow blossoms. The green of the rosettes is not always the same shade; it may be lighter or darker, sometimes grey, blue-green or even pale with darker tips.

In rock gardens it is recommended to grow several species together, amidst stones as well as in narrow gaps in walls, where they spread joining the separate stones into a harmonious whole.

The Cobweb Houseleek *(S. arachnoideum)* forms small rosettes of many leaves and bears rose-red flowers. This species and its red-leaved varieties are particularly attractive on pale, limestone rocks. *S. ornatum* forms larger rosettes that are red in the centre with green tips.

Most species of *Sempervivum* grow in the wild in lime-free soils and in cultivation any light well drained garden soil will do. They can also be planted on the top of walls, where they grow well in very little soil. They also require a position in the sun.

Propagation is by planting individual leaf rosettes which soon grow roots and also by seed. Low carpeting rock plants make good companions.

# Mountain Soldanella  Primulaceae
*Soldanella montana*

Soldanellas are among the loveliest spring flowerers of the Primrose family. They have circular, leathery, dark green leaves. In early spring they bear fringed bell-shaped flowers on short stems.

The Mountain Soldanella *(S. montana)* grows freely in the limestone Alps, its natural distribution extending eastwards through the Carpathians. The plants reach a height of about 8 inches (20 cm.) and grow on the edges of coniferous woods in damp soil, covered with moss.

Another member of this genus is the Alpine Soldanella *(S. alpina)*. It also is a native of southern Europe and the Balkans. A small plant growing to a height of only 2 to 6 inches (5 to 15 cm.). It bears blue-violet, funnel-shaped flowers in April and May. In the mountains it is found at very high altitudes, up to 9,000 feet (3,000 metres).

Soldanellas do well in rock gardens in moist postions, shaded or turned away from the sun, in porous, soils with an admixture of peat or best of all soil from a leafy woodland with added clay. They do not like constant shade. If conditions are suitable they sow themselves freely.

Propagation is easy by seed, but is also possible by division.

Good companions are early flowering, not too vigorous Hepaticas *(Hepatica triloba)*, Primulas, Lungworts *(Pulmonaria)*, *Dentaria* and also small spring-flowering bulbs.

# Penny Cress                                     Cruciferae

*Thlaspi ochroleucum*

These plants are typical of high mountains and screes but are not so well known as some high alpines and deserve to be included in the rock garden. They are small evergreens, with oval, dark green leaflets, the clumps enveloped with a cloud of flowers in early spring. *T. ochroleucum*, a native of the Balkans, is only 2 to 6 inches (5 to 15 cm.) high with white flowers which later turn yellow.

One of the most often cultivated members of this genus is the Alpine Penny Cress *(T. alpestre)*, 2 to 12 inches (5 to 30 cm.) high, bearing pink-tinged, later white flowers from April till June. Like all other species of *Thlaspi* it is most effective in the rock garden if set out in large numbers.

One of the prettiest species is the Round-leaved Penny Cress *(T. rotundifolium)* of the Alps and Carpathians. This makes congested clumps of circular leaves only 2 to 4 inches (5 to 10 cm.) high, and has pleasantly perfumed red-violet flowers during July and August. *T. stylosum* (syn. *Noccaea stylosa*), a native of the Appennines, is a very small 1 to 2 inches (3 to 6 cm.) high plant forming ground-hugging tufts of hard, dark green leaves. From March till April it bears masses of pale violet, almond scented blossoms borne on the tips of small, short stems. This species is particularly suitable for stony and humus rich soils in positions facing away from the sun.

All the members of this genus require good drainage, otherwise they are greatly damaged and usually die in damp winters.

Propagation is comparatively easy by seed and division of clumps.

## *Trachelium rumelianum*          Campanulaceae

*T. rumelianum* is an interesting and comparatively rare plant not often found in our rock gardens. A native of the Balkans and Greece, it forms woody prostrate bushes with pale green foliage and has violet-blue flowers arranged in spherical clusters.

*Trachelium* is a low, sprawling plant suitable for the rockery, on walls or spaces between stones, which its underground shoots penetrate. Its greenery and profusion of flowers are very decorative in the summer garden. It thrives in a sunny position in loose, porous, lightly moist, loamy-sandy soil with some lime, and is valued for its late flowering (August).

*T. rumelianum* var. *chalcidicum* is a wonderful delicate blue variety.

Another member of the genus is *T. coeruleum* (syn. *Diosphaera coerulea*) of southern Europe bearing heads of pale blue flowers; its height 20 to 40 inches (50 to 100 cm.), however, makes it too tall for the rock garden.

Propagation is generally by seed, but cuttings may be taken occasionaly.

It is very effective together with more delicate, not too invasive rock plants such as *Primula marginata*, *Dianthus neglectus*, *Edraianthus*, and low, neat, ornamental grasses, for example *Festuca*.

# Spiderwort  Commelinaceae
*Tradescantia virginiana*

*T. virginiana*, closely related to the popular *Tradescantia* grown indoors, is a native of North America. It is a tall plant reaching a height of as much as 24 inches (60 cm.) and has a long, uninterrupted flowering period from June till August. It makes congested clumps of nodulated stems with long leaves and thick, terminal clusters of buds which open one after the other. The violet-blue blossoms are short-lived hence the common name Flower of the Day. In *T. virginiana* 'Alba' they are white and somewhat smaller, in *T. virginiana* 'Iris' large, coloured a rich blue, in *T. virginiana* 'Leonore' gentian-blue and in *T. virginiana* 'Purewell Giant' carmine.

The plants like adequate moisture and partial shade and are excellent set out in large numbers along the edge of pools in the company of *Trollius*, the perennial Forget-Me-Nots *(Myosotis)* as well as the Evening Primrose *(Oenothera tetragona)* and also the Blazing Star *(Liatris)*.

Propagation is usually by division or by seed, under favourable conditions they sow themselves.

# Globe Flower                                Ranunculaceae

*Trollius pumilus*

Few know that this genus also embraces quite small plants that are very suitable for the rock garden.

One of the prettiest is *T. pumilus*, native of the Himalayas, reaching a height of only 8 inches (20 cm.). It bears single, yellow flowers, reminiscent of Marsh Marigold in June and July, and is very good in the so-called 'alpine meadows' of the rock garden; also suitable are the somewhat taller, orange-yellow *T. yunnanensis* (syn. *pumilus yunnanensis*) or *T. patulus* a native of Asia Minor and Persia, 12 to 16 inches (30 to 40 cm.) high with half-opened orange flowers.

The smallest member of this genus is *T. acaulis* of the Himalayas, only 4 to 6 inches (10 to 15 cm.) high, with open, golden-yellow flowers.

These species are propagated by seed or by division of the roots during spring or autumn.

Good neighbours are dwarf Buttercups *(Ranunculus)* perennial Forget-Me-Nots *(Myosotis palustris)*, *Thlaspi* and the like.

Besides the foregoing there are also the large flowered species of *Trollius* which should not be lacking in any garden. Those usually found in cultivation are the earlier flowering European species *T. europaeus* and forms and the orange coloured Asiatic species, which may have repeated flowerings until the autumn.

These are best planted in the company of other perennials in the sun as well as light shade in heavy, lime-free soils with ripe humus.

# Tulip  Liliaceae

*Tulipa tarda*

Tulips, especially the botanical species and forms derived from them, are cultivated in our gardens and rock gardens, along with a great number of small bulbous plants. The flowering period begins very early in spring and continues for several weeks. Tulips may remain for several years in one spot without any detrimental effect on flowering. They grow well in the sun and as a rule in light shade also.

*T. tarda* (syn. *dasystemon*), a native of Turkestan, is one of the most rewarding species suitable for rock gardens. Rising from rosettes of leaves is a 4 inches (10 cm.) long stem bearing several pretty yellow flowers in April and May. These are very persistent and very effective in the spring garden. The plant thrives especially in porous, sandy soil.

Another Turkestan species is *T. turkestanica*, a small tulip 8 inches (20 cm.) high, with creamy-yellow flowers, it will even grow under bushes where it spreads freely and in time forms whole carpets.

The wild, so-called botanical Tulips, are very numerous, they differ from the well known, garden species in size, shape of the flowers, colour, foliage and also by the fact that they flower much earlier. Besides the original wild species there are today many new and varied garden forms; some of these are low, almost miniature plants and may have several blossoms on one stem.

# Speedwell  Scrophulariaceae
*Veronica cinerea*

The Speedwells comprise about 150 species, only a few of which are suitable for cultivation in rock gardens. They are perennials and natives of many places, their greatest attraction being the clear blue colour of the flowers.

*V. cinerea*, a native of Greece, is 4 to 5 inches (10 to 12 cm.) high with attractive grey-green foliage, the narrow leaves neatly arranged on prostrate stems. It spreads well and bears blue to pinkish-blue flowers in May and June. It likes a soil that is not too rich and a dry position in full sun.

*V. rupestris* (syn. *prostrata*), a native of Asia Minor is another very lovely and modest Speedwell. It attains a height of only 2 to 4 inches (5 to 10 cm.) and makes prostrate mats of fine leaves covered in June with brilliant ultramarine flowers.

Besides the type plant there are also several garden varieties, e.g. the white *V. cinerea* 'Alba', the blue-white *V. cinerea* 'Pallida', and the pink *V. cinerea* 'Rosea'.

None of these Speedwells have any special requirements as to soil or situation.

Propagation is generally by division, but in some species by seed or cuttings.

Good neighbours are Candytuft *(Iberis saxatilis)*, Mouse-ear Chickweed *(Cerastium columnae)* Campion *(Silene alpestris)*, yellow Sun Rose *(Helianthemum)*, Milfoil *(Achillea tomentosa)*, Pinks *(Dianthus plumarius)* and other similar plants.

# Horned Violet  Violaceae

*Viola cornuta*

The type plant is a native of the Pyrenees where it makes large mats 8 to 10 inches (20 to 25 cm.) high and bears a profusion of blue to dark violet flowers with small, yellow centre. However, only garden forms are found in cultivation.

These are very valuable plants in the garden and rockery especially for their exceptionally long flowering period and low growth. They can be used both in edgings and in the front lines of borders. They are intolerant of full sun but in shaded spots the flowering is far more meager.

The commonest of the well-known forms are 'Ardwell Gem' — a magnificent canary yellow with dark centre, 'Blauwunder' — bright blue tinged with violet, and with a very lengthy flowering period, 'Hansa' — a well known and hardy, blue-violet form, and 'Ruhm von Aalsmeer' — a new Dutch form with medium-sized, dark purplish-violet flowers with blue sheen.

The plants should be cut back completely after flowering and top dressed with good soil, thus attaining repeated flowering. All the varieties bear blossoms from May till August and longer.

Violets do well in any loose garden soil in a sunny position. Permanent damp is harmful.

Propagation is by division and cuttings, in some forms also by seed.

Violets are effective planted between spring perennials, *Iris pumila*, Milfoil *(Achillea)*, Candytuft *(Iberis sempervirens)*, low-growing Chalk Plants *(Gypsophila)*, Madwort *(Alyssum)*, *Geum*, Rock Cress *(Arabis)*, *Primula elatior* and others.

# Alpine Catchfly  Cariophyllaceae
*Viscaria alpina*

A native of the high Alps, Pyrenees and Apennines, *V. alpina* is one of the smallest species of this genus, forming a congested rosette of dark green leaves. Attaining a height of 2 to 6 inches (5 to 15 cm.) the plants make small tufts and bear carmine, pink and white flowers in April and May.

This delicate and modest dwarf alpine does best on lime-free soil in a sunny position, in joins between the stones or in stone debris amidst smaller rock plants. It is popular with gardeners for its low growth but at low altitudes older plants tend to disappear from our rockeries after flowering. In a propitious environment, however, it usually spreads itself by self-sown seedlings.

The soil should be moist, loamy-sandy with peat.

One of the best known forms is *V. vulgaris* 'Splendens Plena' (syn. *Lychnis viscaria* 'Splendens Plena'). It is a double variety of the widespread wild species found on meadows in central Europe and bears a great profusion of fairly large, brilliant carmine-pink flowers in May and June.

Viscarias are popular plants for borders, flower beds and larger rock gardens. Together with suitably selected neighbours they form a bright and colourful pattern. Good companions are blue Speedwells, Mouse-ear Chickweed *(Cerastium biebersteinii)*, *Chrysanthemum maximum* and other perennials with the same flowering period.

# Cow's Walk                              Scrophulariaceae

*Wulfenia carinthiaca*

*Wulfenia*, natives of the Alps and the Himalayas are interesting plants. In the wild they occur in damp, mountain meadows over a limestone foundation. Their broad rosettes of glossy, dark green leaves are very decorative. The flowers, borne in June and July, are blue with a violet tinge. The best known species is *W. carinthiaca*, which reaches a height of 6 to 9 inches (15 to 20 cm.) when in flower, also has a white form — *W. carinthiaca* 'Alba'.

One *Wulfenia* species found only rarely in cultivation is *W. amherstiana* of the Himalayas, attaining a height of no more than 6 to 8 inches (15 to 20 cm.) and bearing bright violet flowers. Another is *W. baldacci* of Albania, also only 6 inches (15 cm. )high and bearing lilac-blue flowers in a loose spike in June and July.

These plants like loose, slightly alkalic soil, rich in humus and mixed with stone debris, and do not tolerate larger concentrations of lime in the soil. The best position is one turned away from the sun. A good supply of water is required in summer, whereas in winter the soil should be dry.

In rock gardens *Wulfenia* should be planted in north-facing situations, best of all in fissures between stones or in the same sort of spot as *Ramonda*.

Propagation is by division of larger clumps in the spring or by seed also sown in spring.

# INDEX OF ENGLISH NAMES

| | |
|---|---|
| Anemone, Japanese | 78 |
| — Snowdrop | 80 |
| Aster, Alpine | 90 |
| Avens | 142 |
| — Mountain | 124 |
| | |
| Balloon Flower | 188 |
| Bell Flower | 100 |
| Bitter-root | 168 |
| Buttercup, Alpine | 202 |
| | |
| Candytuft, Evergreen | 158 |
| — Lebanon | 68 |
| Catchfly, Alpine | 236 |
| Chalk Plant | 146 |
| Chickweed | 104 |
| Columbine | 82 |
| Cow's Walk | 238 |
| Cowslip, American | 118 |
| Crane's Bill | 140 |
| Cress, Penny | 222 |
| — Purple Rock | 96 |
| — Rock | 84 |
| — Store | 68 |
| | |
| Daisy, Blue | 144 |
| — Michaelmas | 92 |
| Dragon's head | 122 |
| | |
| Edelweiss | 166 |
| | |
| Flax | 172 |
| Fleabane | 128 |
| | |
| Garland Flower | 114 |
| Gentian | 136 |
| Globe Flower | 228 |
| Goat's Beard | 94 |
| Gold Dust | 72 |
| Golden Drop | 176 |
| Grass, Whitlow | 104 |
| | |
| Heath, Sea | 76 |
| Heather | 126 |
| Houseleek | 218 |
| | |
| Iris, Dutch | 162 |
| | |
| Jasmine, Rock | 76 |
| | |
| Lavender | 164 |
| Leopards Bane | 120 |
| London Pride | 212 |
| | |
| Milfoil | 66 |
| Milkwort | 134 |
| Mouse-ear, Chickweed Alpine | 104 |
| | |
| Onion, Flowering | 70 |
| Orchid, Lady's Slipper | 112 |
| Oxlip, Bardfield | 192 |
| | |
| Paeony | 178 |
| Pasque Flower | 196 |
| Phlox | 182 |
| Pink | 116 |
| — Moss | 184 |
| — Sea | 86 |
| Poppy, Alpine | 180 |
| Primrose, Evening | 174 |
| — Pyrenean | 200 |

| | | | |
|---|---|---|---|
| Rampion, Horned | 186 | Squill | 214 |
| Rockfoil | 208 | St. John's Wort | 156 |
| Rose | 204 | Startwort, Summer | 128 |
| — Christmas | 150 | Stonecrop | 216 |
| — Lenten | 152 | | |
| — Sun | 148 | Thrift | 86 |
| | | Thrift, Prickly | 64 |
| Saxifrage, Silver | 208 | Toadflax | 170 |
| Sea Heath | 76 | Tulip | 230 |
| Shooting Star | 118 | | |
| Slipper Flower | 170 | Violet, Dog's Tooth | 132 |
| Soapwort | 206 | — Horned | 234 |
| Soldanella, Mountain | 220 | | |
| Speedwell | 232 | Wormwood | 88 |
| Spiderwort | 226 | | |
| Spurge | 134 | Yarrow | 66 |

# INDEX OF LATIN NAMES

| | | | |
|---|---|---|---|
| Acantholimon glumaceum | 64 | Dracocephallum austriacum 'Rubrum' | 122 |
| Achillea tomentosa | 66 | Dryas octopetala | 124 |
| Aethionema warleyense | 68 | | |
| Allium ostrowskianum | 70 | | |
| Alyssum saxatile | 72 | Erica carnea | 126 |
| Anacyclus depressus | 74 | Erigeron aurantiacus | 128 |
| Androsace chamaejasme | 76 | Erinus alpinus | 130 |
| Anemone japonica | 78 | Erythronium dens-canis | 132 |
| Anemone silvestris 'Grandiflora' | 80 | Euphorbia myrsinites | 134 |
| Aquilegia discolor | 82 | | |
| Arabis albida | 84 | Frankenia laevis | 76 |
| Armeria maritima | 86 | | |
| Artemisia lanata | 88 | Gentiana acaulis | 136 |
| Aster alpinus | 90 | Gentiana sino-ornata | 138 |
| Aster amellus | 92 | Geranium argenteum | 140 |
| Astilbe chinensis 'Pumila' | 94 | Geum chiloense | 142 |
| Aubrietia deltoidea | 96 | Globularia trichosantha | 144 |
| | | Gypsophila paniculata 'Rosenschleier' | 146 |
| Bergenia cordifolia | 98 | | |
| Calceolaria biflora | 170 | Heliantheum apenninum | 148 |
| Campanula bellidifolia | 100 | Helleborus atrorubens | 152 |
| Campanula portenschlagiana | 102 | Helleborus niger | 150 |
| Cerastium alpinum | 104 | Hepatica triloba | 154 |
| Clematis alpina | 106 | Hypericum rhodopaeum | 156 |
| Cortusa matthioli | 108 | | |
| Cyclamen europaeum | 110 | Iberis sempervirens | 158 |
| Cypripedium calceolus | 112 | Incarvillea delavayi | 160 |
| | | Iris × hollandica | 162 |
| Daphne cneorum | 114 | Lavandula officinalis | 164 |
| Dianthus alpinus | 116 | Leontopodium alpinum | 166 |
| Dodecatheon meadia | 118 | Lewisia cotyledon | 168 |
| Doronicum columnae | 120 | Linaria alpina | 170 |
| Draba aizoides | 104 | Linum salsoloides | 172 |

| | | | |
|---|---|---|---|
| Oenothera missouriensis | 174 | Saxifraga marginata | 210 |
| Onosma albo-roseum | 176 | Saxifraga x paulinae | 210 |
| | | Saxifraga umbrosa | 212 |
| Paeonia tenuifolia | 178 | Scilla sibirica | 214 |
| Papaver alpinum kerneri | 180 | Sedum spurium | |
| Phlox divaricata | 182 | 'Superbum' | 216 |
| Phlox subulata | 184 | Sempervivum | |
| Phyteuma scheuchzeri | 186 | arachnoideum | 218 |
| Platycodon grandiflorum | 188 | Sempervivum ornatum | 218 |
| Primula auricula | 190 | Soldanella montana | 220 |
| Primula elatior | 192 | | |
| Primula rosea | 194 | Thlaspi ochroleucum | 222 |
| Pulsatilla vulgaris amoena | 196 | Townsendia formosa | 202 |
| Pulsatilla vulgaris | | Trachelium rumelianum | 224 |
| 'Slavica' | 198 | Tradescantia virginiana | 226 |
| | | Trollius pumilus | 228 |
| Ramonda pyrenaica | 200 | Tulipa tarda | 230 |
| Ranunculus montanus | 202 | | |
| Rosa multiflora | | Veronica cinerea | 232 |
| 'Sweet Pink' | 204 | Viola cornuta | 234 |
| | | Viscaria alpina | 236 |
| Saponaria ocymoides | 206 | | |
| Saxifraga aizoon | 208 | Wufenia carinthiaca | 238 |